CONNECTIONS

barcelona
mamas
in biz

SEEN HEARD SUPPORTED

Imprint: Alaya Books

Cover illustration by Dan Negrut

Cover design by Amy Piumarta and Natalia Hooker

Interior formatting by Alaya Books

In memory of Judi Oshowole.

Contents

Foreword

I have met very few people whom I would call a force of nature. Amy Piumarta is one of them. It's her combination of focus, boundless energy, and an effervescence that comes bubbling out and spills over, stimulating the very air that surrounds her.

We met as neighbours in Barcelona, in the typical building where everyone is polite, but no one really talks to each other. We decided to have tea together and that eventually evolved into a deep friendship that came to feel like family.

It has been my privilege to see Amy evolve into the person she wants to be and is; extraordinary as a mother, I've seen her teaching her boys to show kindness to everyone they meet. I continue to delight in her use of creative, silly euphemisms for swear words that evolve, her extraordinary fashion sense, and her heartfelt joy in the life she is living. And she knows how to have fun – never underestimate the value of fun.

Amy is a born connector, intuitively knowing how to make things happen by recognising each person she meets as an added wealth and each situation as an opportunity, instead of a possible impediment. She has a generosity of spirit and a deepfelt dedication to giving back to the world and all of us, its inhabitants. That commitment led her to fully explore where she both wanted to be and needed to be. With dedication and hard work, she began to build, creating a business that marked the birth and continuing evolution of Mamas in Biz.

This publication is a testament to the kaleidoscope of women she has reached out to and to the community she has created where they are both nurtured and nurturers. Their vastly diverse constellations of backgrounds and interests are the wealth that Amy identified and valued as their strengths. She was conscious of how all of these voices together have a purpose that give them a visibility in the magnificent, multilingual city of Barcelona, where individuals might flounder and fall through the cracks. Now there is a net, that is also a trampoline, and it knows no boundaries.

Katherine Slusher

Katherine Slusher is a writer and curator based in Barcelona. She has a Master of Arts in Museum Studies from Syracuse University and a PhD in Art History from the University of Barcelona. Among her publications, Katherine is the author of a dual biography entitled *Lee Miller and Roland Penrose: The Green Memories of Desire* (Prestel, London).

mamas you are seen, heard and supported. mamas you are seen, heard and supported.

barcelona

mamas

in biz

AMY PIUMARTA

"Many mothers are feeling how I once felt – isolated, overwhelmed, trying to juggle it all."

This book is deeply personal to me because it is dedicated to my dear friend, Judi. Her dream was always to write her story, but she passed before she could make that happen. When she died in July 2024, the realisation that she never got to tell her story hit me very hard. Not long after, I began to feel this quiet, internal whisper: *You need to tell her story.*

At first, I didn't know how, when, or even where to begin. Then one day it became clear – I needed to create a book and dedicate it to Judi. *Connections* is my way of honouring her.

I'm not a writer, and I had no idea how to start creating a book, so I reached out to fellow Mamas in Biz member Natalia, founder of Alaya Books. She immediately loved the idea and knew exactly what to do.

Thank you Natalia, for believing in this project and guiding it to life.

This is a pure love project: born from hours of devotion, from the courage of so many women who have shared their truths, and from the collective energy that carried it through every stage of creation. Bringing it to life has been the greatest honour.

Before I go any further, I'd like to invite you to pause and think back to your own childhood. What did you dream about when you were young? What did you want to be when you grew up? Maybe it was something big, maybe it was something small – but take a moment to remember.

As for me, I was certain I wanted to be a vet because I absolutely adored animals. In fact, nearly everything I did at school seemed to circle back to that theme. I even started a group with my primary school friends in the garden shed at the back of my family home. I called it the 'Animal Club'. We'd meet regularly to talk about anything and everything to do with animals.

I can still picture my mum running down the garden path with a tray of drinks and biscuits. 'Mums', as I call my mum, would pass them to us and then leave us to chat together about our love for our furry, four-legged friends. While my dream of becoming a vet didn't happen, I did hold onto the idea of bringing women together in a group setting. And now, over thirty-five years later, I feel like now I've found my soul's purpose and everything I've done before me has brought me to this place of where I am today. I am still bringing females together, but instead of talking about animals, we focus on our goals, our dreams, and our businesses.

When I met my partner in 2014, everything moved fast. Within the first year, we met, fell in love, had our first child... and then made the massive decision to leave the UK and move abroad. Looking back now, it sounds wild. But at the time, it just felt right. He'd been living in the UK for ten years and was ready for something new. I was in love and wide open to the adventure, even though we barely knew each other. That's the honest truth.

We decided on three cities that we liked: Amsterdam, Barcelona, and Berlin. I'd lived in Berlin before, so we ruled it out. Amsterdam? Beautiful, but the same grey skies as London. So, we picked Barcelona for the sunshine. Pure and simple. And Luc, my partner, already spoke Spanish, so it felt like something we could make work. Now here is the crazy thing, I had never even been to Barcelona. Not once. And two weeks before the move I found out I was pregnant again. So there I was, a brand new mum, in a relationship of just over a year, pregnant, about to leave my whole life behind to start a new one in a city I'd never stepped foot into.

Our belongings in suitcases, a nine-month-old baby, a belly, and a huge leap into the unknown...

While the beginning was intense, this city has become my home. I'm so grateful I took the leap, even if it made no sense on paper. And that's where everything started to shift again. Since moving to Barcelona, I have stepped into a completely new chapter, not just becoming a mother, but also starting to work independently for the first time. My entrepreneurial journey all started in Barcelona, so in more ways than one, I started a completely new life.

I'd been in the beauty industry since I was seventeen and had built a career I loved. I enjoyed the industry, and I'd always been proud of the work I did. But when I moved here, I knew it was going to be difficult to work for someone else. The hours weren't family-friendly, and I couldn't imagine working weekends, late nights, and public holidays while raising two little ones. So I decided to do my own thing. I started offering waxing and other beauty services from home, using the skills I'd built up over the years.

Around the same time, I was offered an opportunity to sell beauty products online through social media. With my background in beauty, it felt like a perfect fit, like a natural transition. It was a business model that worked around my family life and gave me something that was mine. Social media became a huge part of that. Back in London, I never really used social media, maybe just to wish people happy birthday. But soon it became a daily practice. I started showing up, sharing my business, building awareness, and connecting with other people. It became more than just a platform, it was a lifeline. It grounded me. It helped me feel seen and heard in a new country, in a new role. It gave me an identity outside of just being 'mum'.

But as with most things in life, it wasn't all smooth sailing. Working for myself had its perks, but it could also be isolating. I was at home most of the time, surrounded by boys – my partner and two sons. I love them deeply, but I missed female energy. I needed conversations with women who understood the juggle. I felt lonely, like I was doing it all on my own.

I remember having a beautiful chat with a dear friend of mine, Julia. I call her Miss Sunshine because that's exactly what she is. We were sitting on a bench in *Parc de la Ciutadella*, in the centre of the city, we were right in front of a beautiful fountain in the middle of the park. It was one of those chats where you talk about life, intentions, and what you want your future to look like. I told her I had an idea:

"I want to create a space for women, especially mothers, who are running their own businesses. A place where we can come together, support each other, and feel like we aren't doing it all alone. Somewhere we can be seen, heard, and understood."

Her reply was simple, "I love it!"

On my birthday, 22nd of October, 2021, Mamas in Biz was born. That's when the idea really came to life. It started small, just a concept and a bit of a plan, but something inside me knew this was needed. Not just for me, but for so many women. One thing I was sure about from the beginning was that all I needed was 'connection'. Real connection and community. From that moment on, I knew I just needed to start connecting with women.

I went back to social media, this time to a Facebook group. I posted: "Are there any other mums out there with an independent business who'd like to be part of a WhatsApp group?" The response was incredible. Women started reaching out straight away. I began doing connection calls with each of them, just to make sure they were genuine and to hear a little bit about their stories. Within a few weeks, there were around twenty women in the group, so I invited them all to my home for our very first networking event. It reminded me of the Animal Club days, and despite being all grown up, we were still young girls at heart with dreams that we wanted to manifest.

It was a truly a wonderful event. We'd just come out of the pandemic. After being locked in our homes for so long, suddenly I had strangers in my living room – hugging, laughing, sitting close together, sharing stories. The energy was so warm and welcoming, and I can still feel the magic from that day. It's etched in my memory – the smiles, the joy, the sense of finally being around people who understood one another.

Many of the women had products to sell, so not long after, I put together our first pop-up market. A few weeks later, we did not one but two Christmas markets. And from there, it just kept growing. More women joined. I kept doing the connection calls. We began hosting workshops, monthly pop-up markets, and events, as well as workshops hosted and run by the women themselves – giving them space to lead and shine. I started offering online support, visibility for their businesses, and more in-person opportunities too.

Over time, it continued to evolve into something really special. Now, Mamas in Biz is a subscription-based community with an ever-growing hub of support. We offer online coworking, monthly networking sessions, coaching calls, and a place to showcase what you do both digitally and face-to-face. We've grown to over 140 women from all walks of life, and the energy we have is real, raw, and beautifully diverse.

The truth is, many of the women who join this community are feeling how I once felt – isolated, overwhelmed, trying to juggle it all. They're managing home life, kids, meals, shopping, school runs, sleepless nights... and running a business, often by themselves. Social media, marketing, follow-ups, admin – it's a lot. And it's even more when you feel like you're doing it alone. That's where Mamas in Biz steps in. This space gives women the support they need and deserve. The connections, the visibility, and the encouragement. Real women who get it.

If you're wondering what really happens when women join this community.... let me tell you. Yes, they gain visibility. Yes, they grow their businesses. But the real transformation? That's in how they start showing up differently.

I've seen women who were terrified of speaking on camera, gain confidence and start showing up online via video and even go on to host their own events. Women who felt like they didn't belong online begin sharing their stories boldly and creating an audience who relate to their content. Women who had ideas bubbling quietly inside them finally take action, because they were met with encouragement, not competition.

And it's not just about business. It's about friendships too. Deep, beautiful connections have formed through this network, the kind where you feel truly seen and understood. The kind where someone sends a voice note just to check in. Or turn up to support your event without being asked. Or dances with you at an occasion like you've known each other forever.

What I've come to realise is that Mamas in Biz isn't about *business first*. It's about *connection first*. And when women feel connected, they rise. Their confidence increases. Their creativity flows. Their sense of possibility expands. From there, the visibility comes. The clients come. The momentum builds.

And we have fun along the way. We really do. It's not all strategy and structure, sometimes it's laughter, music, messy moments, and dancing like nobody's watching. Because life is short, motherhood is intense, and running a business can be heavy if you let it. So we make space for joy. We celebrate small wins, and we remind each other not to take it all too seriously.

I still do the same video calls I did at the beginning, and they will always be one of my favourite parts of this journey, because that is when I truly begin the connection. They remind me why this started Mamas in Biz in the first place. I do my best to keep in touch with every woman, to follow up, to hold space, and to make sure she feels supported from the moment she joins.

We're constantly evolving as a group, growing not just our businesses, but ourselves. And I truly believe that what you put into something, you get back. That's the energy we work with here.

As I've read through these stories, the chapters of our book, I've been blown away by the honesty, the variety, and the depth of what's been shared. These women have opened up their lives, shared their truths, and shown us what resilience looks like in real time. I've adored finding out more about them, and I know that as you read them, something will ignite within you too. Some stories will feel relatable, others may inspire you or reassure you that you're on the right track. Every one of them carries heart, courage, and truth. And of course, we have the very special chapter at the end, a short biography of the late, Judi Oshowole, written by her life partner, Ruairí Ó Donnchadha.

Thank you for reading, and for being part of this journey with us.

ALLISON PULLEN

Why Barcelona?

When we moved to Barcelona in 2015, it was supposed to be a two-year plan. You might not believe that if you met me now, but I was convinced I'd just live in Barcelona for a while, and then return to my house in the town of Doylestown, Pennsylvania, a wiser and better person.

We'd been in Barcelona for maybe a week when my husband turned to me and said, only half joking, "If you want to go back, you can have the kids and the house, but I'm staying here."

And honestly? It wasn't a hard decision.

My connection to this city began long before I ever set foot in it; before I was even born. My great-grandparents were raised in Barcelona and immigrated to New York over a century ago. Throughout my childhood, we had visits from distant cousins I could hardly communicate with. I remember watching my grandmother's face light up whenever she spoke with them in Catalan. Even without understanding a word, or knowing that Catalan was a separate language from Spanish spoken in Catalunya, I could feel the warmth of those conversations. That joy sparked a desire to learn Spanish and to understand the stories behind those bright eyes.

In 1996, I spent one month in southern Spain on a study abroad experience with my college. Every city I visited in Spain deepened my love for the country, its culture, and its people. On the final weekend of that month abroad, I took a flight to Barcelona to stay with one of my cousins. I loved everything about it – the energy, the architecture, the sea, and I had a sense of familiarity in a place that was technically foreign to me. I left with a promise to myself that I would come back, for longer.

Of course, life has a way of rewriting your plans. I built a career, got married, bought a house, and had children. But the dream never faded, and fortunately, my husband was on board too. Eventually, my husband and I decided it was time. We'd take a break from work, enrol the kids in a local school in Barcelona, immerse ourselves in Spanish, and travel across Europe. It would be a family adventure.

When I announced my move to Barcelona, many friends and family thought I was crazy. But when they came to visit, they got it. The beautiful, wide avenues with modernist architecture, the narrow alleyways of the Gothic Quarter, and over 300 days of sunshine a year were some of the obvious attractions. And as you spend more time in the city, you discover the less obvious aspects. You see families gathering for a meal together every Sunday. You see grandparents pushing their grandchildren in strollers down the street and playing with them in parks. You see friends mingling on a sunny terrace after work for a drink before going home to prepare dinner. You see the love and kindness between all of the people.

Now, this is my home. It's my family's home. My children were six and nine when we moved here, so they created their core memories in Barcelona. When people ask why I stayed, I always tell them it's not just because of one thing. It's the markets, the neighbourhoods, the architecture, the people, the history, and of course the weather – all woven together into something I can't quite define but can absolutely feel.

For those of us who are immigrants, we try to emulate the locals. We don't have an extended family here, so we create our own. Moving abroad is a lesson in itself. You learn what you really value in life, and you cling to that. We discovered that there are many other families here that have the same values as us. We just all had to leave home to find each other.

Barcelona has a special feeling. When I walk down the street I feel the history and modern world combining to make something fabulous. People dress like they care how they look, but they're not trying to compete with anyone. They're fashionable without sacrificing comfort and practicality. As an outsider, it's easy to see how integral family is in Catalan culture. Grandparents care for grandchildren while parents are at work. Children hold their parents' hands for many more years than they do in the United States. Women link arms with each other, teenage boys and men walk down the street with their arms around each other too, and the elderly are very respected and well looked after.

In fact, since I have such a love for Barcelona, and I love sharing it with others, I started a business that embraces this passion. I have always believed you should be passionate about your work. That's why *Spanish Wanderlust* was born. I lead the private tours and plan the itineraries that I would want if I were a visitor. Let me share with you some of the highlights that I notice as a foreigner living in Barcelona.

The Neighbourhoods: A City of Many Villages

One of the first things you notice here is that Barcelona is a patchwork of distinct neighbourhoods ('*barrios*'), each with its own rhythm and soul. Here's a taste of a few.

The Gothic Quarter, with its narrow labyrinth of medieval streets, is like stepping back in time. Hidden courtyards, whimsical gargoyles, and cafés that seem to have existed forever wait around every corner. Just next door is El Born, where chic boutiques and wine bars spill onto the streets, and there's always a sense that something delightful is about to happen, and it is. From talented buskers to regular street festivals, it's pure magic.

Then you have the bright, airy grid of the Eixample, with its elegant modernist buildings, wide boulevards, and endless balconies overflowing with plants. Gràcia feels like a small town inside the city, bohemian and creative, with plazas full of neighbours chatting into the night. Barceloneta, the old fishing quarter, still holds the salty charm of its maritime roots, with the bonus of being on the sea. Once an industrial hub, Poblenou now blends creative studios, modern architecture, and a long sandy beach with the relaxed, local vibe of its lively *Rambla*. Sarrià, my neighborhood, is a former village with tree-lined streets, elegant boutiques, and family-run shops with a small-town charm just minutes from the city centre. And the list goes on. Each *barrio* offers a slightly different version of Barcelona, so you can feel that you have discovered a different place, but it's only five minutes away.

A Feast for the Senses: The Markets

If I could take a newcomer to only one kind of place in the city, it would be the markets. Barcelona's public markets aren't just where you buy groceries. They are the beating heart of the community.

The most famous is *La Boqueria* on La Rambla, a kaleidoscope of colours and aromas bustling with both locals and tourists. But the magic of the markets isn't limited to this one. Each *barrio* has their own, all with unique vendors and vibes.

Here, shopping for food becomes a conversation with the fishmonger about the best way to cook today's catch or with the fruit seller who insists you sample a ripe cherry because it's in season. It's a place to develop relationships, practice the language, try new foods, and even learn new recipes.

Architecture That Makes You Look Up

Barcelona's architecture is one of its most enchanting features. Of course, Gaudí's works steal the spotlight: the dreamlike *Sagrada Família*, the fantastical curves of *Casa Batlló*, and the colourful mosaics of *Park Güell*. But there's so much more. Beyond its modernist icons, Barcelona's architecture also fuses with Gothic, Baroque, Neoclassical, and contemporary.

Even after years here, I still pause mid-walk to take in the way light hits a façade, or the detail of an iron balcony railing. This is a place where beauty lives in the everyday.

Food You Will Fall For

Barcelona is a feast for the senses, and its food and tapas are reason enough to fall in love with the city. Begin with *pan con tomate*, rustic bread rubbed with ripe tomato, olive oil, and salt – the simplest but most satisfying dish you'll remember forever. Then try a *tortilla de patatas*, a comforting Spanish omelette made with eggs, potatoes, and sometimes onions. Indulge in *jamón ibérico*, Spain's prized cured ham, sliced paper-thin so it melts in your mouth. For something with a gentle kick, order *patatas bravas*, crispy potatoes topped with a slightly spicy sauce made with aioli and paprika that's as addictive as it is simple. And finally, savor *fideuá*, a Catalan cousin of paella made with short noodles instead of rice, usually brimming with fresh seafood.

The People and the Pulse

What truly makes Barcelona special are its people. There's a warmth here, a willingness to help, to connect, to make space for you in their circle, that can turn a foreign city into a home. The Catalan sense of community is strong, and while it may take time to be fully embraced, once you are, it's genuine and lasting.

This spirit spills into the streets during festivals, when music, dancing, and human towers take over the plazas. It's in the way neighbours greet each other daily, in the afternoon *vermut*, and in late-night conversations over wine. Local pride is displayed in the city's traditions, such as when young and old come together for Sardana dancing or parades with giants and drums.

Why Families Choose Barcelona

It's no surprise that so many families from around the world find themselves not just visiting Barcelona but planting roots here. For mothers especially, the lifestyle offers something rare: a balance between work and life, ambition and joy. Children grow up surrounded by art, music, languages, and history, and still have the freedom to run barefoot on the beach.

For entrepreneurs, the city offers endless inspiration. There's a strong network of creative, motivated people who support each other, whether they're launching businesses, balancing family life, or both. The pace of life allows for moments – coffee in the sun before a meeting, a spontaneous chat with a neighbour, a walk through the park to clear your head that can spark ideas and nourish your spirit.

And then there's the everyday beauty. Waking up to the sound of church bells, grabbing fresh bread from the bakery on the corner, working from a café with sunny views of modernist buildings, and the Mediterranean Sea at your doorstep. Barcelona isn't just a place to live; it's a place to feel alive.

To me there is no question as to why all the incredible women who have shared their personal journeys in this book have found home here. Barcelona is truly unique and has something for everyone.

Allison Pullen
@livespanishwanderlust
www.spanishwanderlust.com

MARINA KUPERMAN VILLATORO

"Where are you REALLY from?"

"Where are you from?"

Ah yes. *The* question. The one I've been asked roughly seventy-two times a week since moving to Barcelona in 2022.

And I'm not alone. In a city powered by networking events and wine-fuelled meetups, "Where are you from?" is the unofficial handshake. It's harmless. Friendly. A casual little icebreaker.

Unless you're me.

Most people toss out a quick one-word answer: "Canada." "Argentina." "Australia." Then they move on to tapas or more wine.

Me? I freeze. I glitch. I spiral into an existential crisis. Because the truth is... I have no idea how to answer that question without sounding like a monologue from a Netflix docuseries.

To date, I've lived in *eight* countries and over *forty* different cities. Yes, forty. And every place comes with its own nosy FAQ.

Take New York City. No one there cares what country you're from, only if you live 'in the city' or God forbid, across from any of the bridges or tunnels connecting into Manhattan (twenty-five in total). The real interrogation goes like this:

1. "Where do you live?"
2. "What do you do?"
3. "How many hours a week do you work?"

Answer wrong, say "Brooklyn, freelance, twenty-five hours", and boom, you've just been socially deported to Jersey with the other bridge-and-tunnel casualties.

I didn't love New York. But that's a different memoir. Probably written in italics.

In Guatemala and Costa Rica, where my husband and I spent twenty years, nobody asked, "Where are you from?" If you spoke English without a British accent, you were labelled *gringa* and tossed in the generic USA bin. Canadians took this especially hard. Sorry, eh.

Instead, people asked:

1. "Why did you move here?" or
2. "How did you end up here?"

Reasonable questions. No identity crisis required.

So why does *this* one: "Where are you from?" throw me into a mental PowerPoint presentation every time?

Because my origin story includes USSR passports, smuggled goodbyes, nervous breakdowns, and a cast of characters that includes a USSR colonel, thirty bunkmates, and some very stressed-out Soviets.

Let's rewind.

Odessa, Ukraine (part of the Soviet Bloc), 1978. I was five. My parents and I fled the Soviet Union, part of a select group allowed to leave at the time: Soviet Jews. Not Soviets. Not Ukrainians. Not Russians. Just... Jews. Didn't matter if you practised Judaism or not. We didn't. And, when you're from a Communist nation, technically, no one should practice any form of religion. Yet our passports had *JEW* stamped in them like we were property. And if you asked my dad, livestock got treated better.

At the border, they didn't just check our papers. They *ripped them up.* Gone. Just like that. One second we were Soviet citizens. The next, stateless refugees with eight suitcases, $400, and no idea where we were headed. Other than firstly heading to Vienna, for a quick stopover before going on to Rome.

Rome was where the visa game began. You didn't show up with a destination. You showed up and *waited.* The 'invite visa', your golden ticket to a new life, was issued *there.*

We weren't alone. Over 300,000 Soviet Jews made the same journey, many with less than we had. Jewish organisations around the world helped fund the exodus: transportation, boarding houses, train tickets, and a lot of emotional triage.

Picture it: thirty anxious, scared strangers of all ages to a room, one bathroom, zero privacy. This was how life looked in Rome, where we were communally housed. And in the meantime, three questions floated constantly through the air:

1. "Where do you want to end up?"

2. "Did you get your visa yet?"
3. "What country did you finally get your visa to?"

It was like *Survivor: Soviet Jewry Edition*. Everyone praying to be voted into the USA.

Israel was Plan Z. It was always there for you, but came with strings: two years on a kibbutz, instant citizenship, and mandatory military service for your kids. New families (like mine) weren't thrilled about the kibbutz life and definitely not the army clause. So we clung to rumours, favours, and distant family friends. Anything that might earn us a golden ticket to the United States.

Unlike most families who managed to emigrate with a trail of relatives in tow; parents, grandparents, uncles, siblings, and cousins, we had to leave behind the two most important people in my life at the time. My maternal grandparents.

Yes, we were *JEWS*, stamped obnoxiously inside our Soviet passports in block capitals the size of a headline. But my grandfather had somehow defied gravity, pulled off a miracle: he was the only Jewish colonel in the Soviet Army. A coveted, nearly impossible role. One that had never been offered to a Jew before, and probably wouldn't be again.

And then his daughter and her family decided to leave.

If the government caught wind that a member of his family was defecting to the enemy, the United States, it would destroy them. Career, pension, social standing, and secret heartbreak. Gone. Worse, they would be branded as traitors.

My mother had to sit down with her own parents and explain this. The decision broke them. They blamed my father, of course. It was easier to point the finger at someone.

Against all that he believed, and all that he worked so hard for, my grandfather quietly retired. A staged farewell. On paper, it looked voluntary. In reality, it was a shield. The only way to protect himself, my grandma, and my uncle (who was also in the Soviet Army), was by absolute silence. No phone calls. No letters. No messages through friends. We had to disappear from their lives. They had to pretend we were already dead. And we had to do the same.

"You're tearing our family apart," my grandmother sobbed as she begged my father. "You're taking her away from us."

By *her*, they meant me. Their first grandchild. And at that moment, their only grandchild.

From the ages of two to four, I lived with my grandparents. My parents were working around the clock, saving for an escape no one was certain would succeed. In those years, my grandparents were my entire world. The arms I ran to when I was scared, the voices that sang me to sleep, the faces I trusted without question.

And now, we had to pretend that none of it had ever existed. Try explaining that to a five-year-old...

For my father, the choice was clear. His side of the family was all gone, dead. Fleeing an antisemitic country was survival, plain and simple.

For my mother, it was a very different story – the decision nearly broke her.

My mother unravelled. In the months before we left, she suffered two complete nervous breakdowns. Each time, she was hospitalised for months at a time. When she was gone, I stayed home with my father, who, buried under black-market bribes, forged paperwork, and an endless gauntlet of bureaucratic traps, barely had time to breathe, let alone care for a small child.

By the time we arrived in Rome, in that communal room pulsing with anxiety, trauma, and complete uncertainty, my mother was emotionally and physically drained. She was sick all the time. Crying constantly. Hollowed out by grief and guilt. The weight she carried bore down on both of us. I felt it, even as a child. It etched itself into me.

The room itself was a pressure cooker of unspoken grief and jittery hope. Parents whispered behind thin curtains. Children clung to toys they hadn't let go of since Vienna. Everyone waiting, and pretending to be strong.

But my mother? She wasn't pretending. She had left her parents behind, alive but unreachable. That grief filled every corner of our bunk and seeped into me. Even as a child, I knew: some goodbyes were too heavy to carry.

We waited three months. Some waited twelve months. Then, jackpot. A friend of a friend in New York vouched for us. Now life was about to truly get started.

New York City, 1983. We became American citizens (naturalised). I had a passport, a Pledge of Allegiance ceremony, and a deeply emotional attachment to shopping malls.

But that still didn't solve the "Where are you from?" riddle. Because I wasn't *really* from the USA. And for the first ten years, no one let me forget it. "Commie" was used more than my name. Bullying with a Cold War twist.

Then came the wanderlust.

Mid-twenties, I landed in Guatemala. Met a guy three hours in. Married him. I'm skipping ahead here, the long version is getting its own epic tome.

Costa Rica was our first stop. Our first son was born there, planting roots I never planned to grow. Then came Guatemala again, my husband's birth country (he's *never* had trouble answering "Where are you from?"). Where our second boy was born. And just like that, twenty years flew by.

When we finally moved to Barcelona, I realised I'd been gone from the United States longer than I'd lived there. The Soviet Union? Gone. Erased. Like it never existed, making "Where are you from?" even more complicated.

I was born outside Odessa. My first language is Russian. But I'm not Russian. Not Ukrainian. And not even the kind of American who owns a Costco membership and has access to Amazon's same-day drone delivery service.

My eldest son feels the same dislocation. Born in Costa Rica. But not *really* Tico. Raised in Guatemala, but only half Guatemalan. The other half? Undefined. Floating.

We're global citizens. No flag. No anthem. Just a colourful, exotic family tree, really weird answers at customs, and newly formed traditions that I wouldn't have any other way.

But the upside? Barcelona gets it. This city is a magnet for the beautifully rootless, the eclectic, the blended cultures, and the ones with origin stories that need footnotes. Here, I don't need to explain. I'm just one of many with a map full of dots and no single pin.

So, "Where am I from?"

Pull up a chair.

Or better yet, grab a wine glass. Let's toast to being the new culture, the new heritage of Global Citizens, and being fully part of the Barcelona tapestry.

Marina Kuperman Villatoro
@marina.kuperman.villatoro

GIULIA MESSINA

"When passion meets purpose, that's when magic happens."

Becoming a mother was the most beautiful, intense, and disorienting experience of my life. My journey didn't start with a positive pregnancy test or a baby in my arms – it began in 2013 when my husband, Christian, and I got married and dreamed of creating a family. At the time, we weren't in a rush. We lived in London, we were in love, and we were soaking in the beauty of shared adventures, weekends away, and long dinners that stretched into the night. The idea of becoming parents felt like a natural continuation of our bond, but not an urgent destination.

And yet, after a few years, something didn't feel quite right. Months went by, then years. Friends were getting pregnant. Families were growing around us. But our family stayed just the two of us. We weren't obsessing, but we started to question – was something wrong?

After a series of inconclusive tests and doctor appointments, the answer was... nothing. Inexplicable reasons. Nothing they could name. And maybe that's the hardest answer of all. The absence of a clear diagnosis left us in limbo, with no direction to move in. But we kept going. We carried this silent grief while trying not to let it shape who we were.

Still, it shaped us in small ways. There were moments of tension – little arguments sparked by frustration and sadness. I was the healthier one, so sometimes the unspoken weight fell heavier on Christian. We tried to stay hopeful, but after two rounds of IVF and no answers, a quiet doubt crept in. Maybe we weren't meant to be parents? Maybe this wasn't our path.

Looking back now, I see things differently. My body wasn't ready. *I* wasn't ready. I wasn't meant to become a mother in London. Everything unfolded the way it did for a reason. At the time, I was trying to control my life – trying to force it into place through IVF, instead of surrendering to its natural rhythm. And when I finally let go, when I embraced life instead of chasing it, that's when it happened.

In 2018, everything began to shift.

We had just returned from a trip to Mexico. There, something awakened in us. We had spent days watching people live at a slower pace – smiling more, worrying less. There was a sense of surrender in the air. That trip changed us. Perhaps life was not meant to be chased, but lived? We looked at each other and knew: it was time. Not for a baby, but for a life change.

We had always dreamed of living in Barcelona. Ever since we met in London, Christian told me he was going to move there. I said, "I'm coming with you." It had everything we wanted: the sea, the sun, a rich culture, and an energy that felt like home. So we decided to stop postponing the life we craved. We moved in December 2018, right before the world came to a halt.

We loved Barcelona. We soaked it in – its colours, its rhythm, the way the sea made everything feel possible. And when COVID forced the world to pause, it also gave us a strange kind of gift: stillness. Life relaxed for a bit. We were home, just the two of us. I started waking up early to do yoga at sunrise. I felt aligned for the first time in along time – calm and grounded. I remember thinking... *I'm ready. I am going to get pregnant.*

In early 2021, just before we were scheduled for our third round of IVF, something shifted in me. It's hard to explain, but I felt it – as if my body whispered: *Get ready*. I had enrolled in a business course – something for myself, a future vision. I had cleared out the second room in our flat, not necessarily for a nursery, but because I felt the need to make room for something. That month, I got pregnant naturally.

We had booked a hotel room to celebrate our anniversary and also because that was the only way to eat at a restaurant in those lockdown days – and I remember sitting on that hotel bed, waiting for Christian to arrive. I held a pregnancy test in my hands, almost in disbelief. I stared at those two lines, not trusting my eyes. I was happy. Overjoyed! I wanted to jump, to scream, to dance. After everything, the years of waiting, wondering, hoping – there it was. Life. Inside me.

I called my best friends with shaky hands and a heart that could barely contain itself. I couldn't wait to tell Christian. So, on the 22nd of February, the anniversary of the day we met and the day he proposed, I gave him the positive pregnancy test as a gift.

But what came next surprised me even more.

Pregnancy, for me, wasn't the glowing, joyous chapter I had always imagined. It was beautiful, yes, but it was also lonely. Deeply lonely. I felt a strong, almost primal need for connection. I craved conversations with other women going through the same changes –physically, emotionally, mentally. I needed to know I wasn't alone in my fears, my hopes, my shifting identity.

During my pregnancy, I experienced a placental abruption and was placed on bed rest for fifteen days. That quiet, uncertain time brought everything into focus. I realised how deeply I needed other women around me. I didn't want to go through this alone – not the pregnancy, not the birth, not the journey into motherhood. I wanted a space where women could meet, talk, and share their truth.

One morning, I woke up at 5 a.m. with a sense of urgency – a moment of clarity that would become a recurring theme in my life. I didn't grab my phone. I picked up a pen and paper and wrote the message that would become the beginning of something much bigger. I had always dreamed of creating a meetup group for pregnant women, but fear had held me back – fear that no one would come. But that morning was different. I wasn't driven by fear. I was driven by purpose. I finally created a meetup group online and slowly women started to join.

When I organised my first gathering, no one came. I sat at the beach alone looking around to see if anyone was coming towards me, but no one did. But I kept going. Then something magical happened: women started to come and the group grew. Ten women, then twenty. Before long, we were sixty. That group saved me. It gave me connection, purpose, and community. Some of my dearest friends today came from that small seed planted at 5 a.m. We met for coffee, shared birth stories, swapped tips on strollers and stretch marks, and cried over our fears about becoming mothers.

But after my daughter, Coral, was born, everything changed again.

Motherhood, as it turns out, is not just a continuation of pregnancy. It is a transformation. A cracking open. A death and a rebirth. I struggled to find time for myself, let alone to coordinate meetups and manage the group. Feeding, sleep schedules, postpartum healing, mental exhaustion... It consumed me.

Organising something for others felt impossible when I could barely organise myself. I had to let it go. Not because I didn't care anymore, but because I was trying to keep my own head above water.

Motherhood forced me to confront parts of myself I had buried: the need to control, the fear of not being enough, the belief that rest was weakness. It taught me that there is immense strength in vulnerability – in asking for help, in showing up messy and unsure but still choosing to connect.

My husband was working in hospitality – gone most evenings and weekends. I was home with our daughter every day, putting her to bed, taking her to nursery. There wasn't much time for myself. No time for spontaneity. I was drowning in love, exhaustion, and the pressure to do everything *right*.

In 2022, we tried sleep training. It worked beautifully – Coral slept twelve hours a night for an entire year. It gave me back a sense of rhythm, even sanity. But in June 2023, we left her with her grandparents for a short trip, and when she came back, everything changed. The nights became a nightmare – broken sleep, long cries, endless rocking. And this time, I didn't have the same reserves. I was depleted.

That is when I started therapy. And that is when the real transformation began.

Therapy cracked me open in ways I hadn't expected. I thought I was going to talk about my daughter. But instead, I started talking about my mother. About inherited patterns. About the pressure to do everything *right*. About the invisible weight of generations of women who had sacrificed themselves silently, believing that is what love looked like.

In those sessions, I began to realise I didn't want to replicate that story. I didn't want to disappear inside motherhood. I wanted to redefine it, on my own terms.

I started making changes – small, but radical for me. I hired a babysitter. Then a cleaner. I carved out hours – actual, non-negotiable hours – for myself. And slowly, I began to feel human again.

In March 2024, I finished a temporary contract working for the Mobile World Congress. It had been a good project, but when it ended, I found myself at a crossroads. Should I go back to corporate life? Update my LinkedIn? Chase job openings that didn't ignite me?

Then one morning – I swear, always at 5 a.m. – I woke up with clarity. I grabbed my journal and started to write. I flipped back through old entries and read something I had written months before:

When passion meets purpose, that's when magic happens.

And I knew. That was it.

It wasn't just a nice idea. It was a calling. I had to create a space for women to come together in the messy, beautiful, and overwhelming journey of motherhood. A space to share, to listen, to learn. A space to be seen. Because I had felt what it was like to scream in a room and feel like no one was listening.

That's why I started *The Real Truth About Motherhood*.

Not just an event. A movement. A mirror. A sanctuary. A space where women could show up and say, *"This is hard,"* and be met with, *"I know."* Where we could talk honestly about guilt, anger, identity loss, joy, rebirth, rage, softness – all of it. Not curated. Not sugar-coated. Just real.

Since then, I've organised powerful events. Each event filled with incredible women, raw conversations, tears, laughter, and the kind of connection that goes beyond networking –it goes straight to the soul.

Since stepping into this purpose, the universe has made it easy. Doors have opened. People have shown up. Opportunities have flowed in with a grace I could have never engineered. It's as if the path was just waiting for me to say *yes*.

And now, I want to help other women do the same. Because I believe that when a woman aligns with her purpose, everything shifts. Not just for her, but for her family, her community, the world. We have to stop trying to be everything to everyone and start asking, *What makes me feel alive?* Then, we give permission for others to do the same.

Being a mother is the hardest, most beautiful thing I've ever done. It breaks you open. It makes you feel things you didn't know were possible. And if you let it, it transforms you.

Today, I still wake up early. But not out of anxiety – out of purpose.

I write. I dream. I plan. I build. I connect with other women who are ready to change the world – one honest conversation at a time.

This is just the beginning. I have a much bigger vision. I know I'm here to bring real change to this world. And I know I'm not alone.

To every mother reading this who feels like she's screaming and no one hears – I hear you.

To the mother who feels like she's lost herself – you're still in there.

To the mother who's ready to turn her story into something bigger – this is your sign.

And motherhood? It's the greatest source of magic I've ever known.

Giulia Messina
@motherhoodrealtruth
www.motherhoodrealtruth.org

ARCHITA SINGH

"I didn't come this far just to come this far."

I didn't hear them cry. That silence still echoes louder than anything I've ever known. The room was full of people – doctors, nurses, machines – but I felt utterly alone. My babies were here, too early, too small, wrapped in tubes and numbers I didn't understand. I wanted to hold them, but my arms were useless, trembling, frozen. I remember thinking: *I am a mother now. Why does it feel like I'm failing already?*

Just days ago, I had imagined a different beginning. I thought I'd be decorating a nursery, choosing names slowly, and holding soft little fingers with laughter around me. Instead, I found myself whispering prayers to blinking monitors and counting grams like gold. They were born at just twenty-six weeks – twins, each weighing less than a bottle of water. And in those first hours, no one could promise me they'd make it through the night.

I sat in the neonatal intensive care unit (NICU), wrapped in silence, unable to cry because if I started, I wouldn't stop. Machines hummed like lullabies from another world. Nurses moved with quiet urgency. I studied every beep, every number, because it felt like the only control I had. My husband sat beside me, his hands clenched, eyes fixed on the incubators. He didn't say much – there were no right words – but his silence matched mine. We were two people breaking quietly beside each other, trying to stay whole for the tiny lives we had created.

One night in the NICU, the lights were dimmed, and everything felt unbearably still. A nurse gently placed both of the babies on my chest together, their tiny bodies nestled against me like fragile hope. They were so small I was afraid my breath would break them. Their skin felt like warm silk, and they trembled with each tiny inhale. I didn't cry, I couldn't. My whole body was holding its breath. I looked down at their faces – my husband's nose, my mother's chin, my own eyes. These were my people. And they were fighting so hard just to be here. I whispered to them, some mixture of apology and promise, and I hoped they knew they were safe.

A few days later, just as I was starting to find a rhythm in the NICU – knowing the nurses' names, reading the monitors with a little less fear – I walked in and saw something that made my heart stop. From the hallway, I noticed a flurry of movement: nurses running, voices raised, blood bags being rushed in, syringes being prepared. I told my husband,

"Someone's baby must be really sick." And then I stepped through the doors and realised it was my son.

He was surrounded by what felt like an army of medical staff. Tiny limbs poked with needles, tubes being adjusted, numbers flashing red. I froze. I didn't even realise I had dropped to the floor until someone pulled me up. That someone was another mother, a woman whose baby had been born at just twenty-four weeks. She looked into my eyes, not with pity, but strength.

She held me by the shoulders and said, "Don't ever enter a NICU crying. If you cry, they cry. If you break, they break. They feel you. They survive if you survive." Then she took my hand and made me promise, promise not to cry in front of my children.

That day, I learned something no doctor could teach: strength is not loud. It is silent, trembling, and necessary.

Through it all, I sometimes felt a strength that didn't come from me alone. There were nights I'd sit by the incubators, or at the kitchen table late at night, and wonder how I was even standing. And in those quiet moments, I'd feel my dad's presence – like he was there, watching me from wherever he is now. He left this world years ago, but I like to think he's still my guardian angel, steadying me through every storm, whispering: *"You've got this."*

Each day was a battle. My daughter, somehow, was recovering faster. She would stabilise more quickly, respond better to the treatments. My son, though, was struggling. He needed more support, more time, more prayers. But even in those early incubators, side by side, I felt something between them. A pull. A strength that wasn't just theirs individually, but shared. It was as though our daughter was lending her strength to her brother, in quiet, invisible ways. Their hands sometimes brushed through the glass walls of their beds. Their breathing synced. And we, as their parents, began to draw strength from them, not the other way around.

Every day, their bond reminded me: this was not just about survival. This was about togetherness, about love showing up in the tiniest, fiercest ways. Our son fought harder because his sister was beside him. And somehow, every day, they both made it.

We eventually made it home. Not the home I had imagined, not yet. But our babies survived, and for that, I was grateful beyond words. Just as we were learning how to live again, how to hold them without wires, how to breathe without fear, we were packing our lives into boxes.

I come from Varanasi, India, a city where life moves with heart – chaotic yet familiar. But at the time my children were born, we were living in Zurich, Switzerland. We had relocated there for my husband's work in IT. We had lived in Barcelona previously and loved it, so when my husband had the opportunity to work in Barcelona again, we decided to take it.

Now we were moving back to Spain, with two babies who had already taught us the meaning of survival. I thought the hard part was over. I thought starting over in a new place would be exhausting, yes, but manageable. My husband and I leaned on each other, sometimes without words, just through shared looks in the middle of another sleepless night. What we didn't know was that just a few months after arriving, the world would shut down.

COVID didn't just close borders; it closed doorways to connection. We were in a new land, where everything felt unfamiliar. No family, no friends, no comfort in routine. But we had each other. Some days, that didn't feel like enough. Other days, it was everything.

In the midst of that silence, between feeds and folded laundry, between breakdowns, I kept to myself and I found myself in the kitchen. Not for fun, not at first. Just to feed us. But even that felt familiar in a world where nothing else did.

I always loved cooking. When I was a child, I used to sit in the kitchen watching my parents cooking, especially my dad. I loved learning, trying new recipes, and making my whole family taste my latest creations.

In Barcelona, I began making the dishes I grew up with. Spices became my therapy – cumin seeds crackling in mustard oil, the scent of fresh spices, the rhythm of kneading dough. These were things my hands remembered, even when my mind felt lost. Cooking wasn't just about food. It was a thread that tied me back to who I was before motherhood, before hospitals, before lockdowns and new languages.

Then one day, someone asked: "Do you sell this?"

I laughed. Me? Sell food? I was just trying to stay sane. But that question planted a seed. When I told my husband, he didn't hesitate. He said, "Why not? You're amazing at this." He helped me pack those first few takeaway food boxes, watched the kids while I prepped orders late at night, and cheered every small success like it was a grand milestone.

And through it all, I felt held – not just by him, but by my mother, my brother, my sister. We were miles apart, in different countries, separated by circumstances beyond our control, but never by love. Every small or big decision, every breakdown or celebration, I called them. They were my constant, my grounding force, my people who held me up even from afar. We fought, we laughed, and we survived together.

As the business began to take shape and I found my rhythm, I was introduced to a local community of mothers, Mamas in Biz. Women who, like me, were juggling diapers and dreams, late-night feeds and early-morning ambition. It felt like a lifeline. I had finally found others who understood the chaos I lived with daily.

In that circle, I found inspiration, learning, and even laughter. We celebrated small wins and held space for one another's doubts. At the end of the day, I was building something not just for that moment, but for the woman I was becoming, and for the little eyes that were watching me do it.

What started as a quiet, home-based comfort turned into something bigger. But with that growth came challenges. I am still struggling to build something that feels real, still looking for the right space and the right investments to take this business to the next level. There are days

I feel like giving up, days when orders are slow or mistakes happen, and doubt whispers louder than confidence. But I also know this: I didn't come this far just to come this far.

I want to take it to a place where it feels full, authentic, meaningful, and rooted in heart, like my home city, Varanasi. A place where my children will walk in and feel proud of what their mother created. Where they'll learn that dreams take time, effort, and belief – especially in yourself.

Varanasi is the kind of place where neighbours are family, and every street corner holds a memory. Women who manage households like CEOs, shopkeepers who remember your name, and chai breaks that turn into therapy sessions. Varanasi shaped me. It taught me that strength doesn't always roar; sometimes, it simmers, like a pot of curry on a low flame.

Bringing that strength with me to new countries was never easy. But I carried it in small ways –in the way I showed up for my children, in the food I made, in the business I dared to dream of.

I still have so much to learn, so much to do. But I am committed. And I believe that one day, this will be more than a small kitchen dream. It will be a legacy of love and resilience.

Now, when I look back – at hospital corridors and silent nights, at lockdown kitchens and packing boxes – I don't see brokenness anymore. I see transformation. I see a woman who didn't know she could survive what she did, who kept showing up even when nothing made sense, who built something from scratch when it would've been easier to walk away.

My children don't remember those early struggles, not the wires or alarms or tears I swallowed – but I do. And I carry them like a hidden medal on my chest. A reminder that motherhood, for me, was never just about birth; it was about rebirth, of myself.

I still dream. I still hustle. Some days I still break. But I rise too. I rise because I have stories to tell, hands to hold, meals to cook, and a legacy I want to leave behind.

I want my children to grow up knowing that strength doesn't always wear armour – it sometimes wears an apron, or smiles through tired eyes, or speaks softly into the night when no one else is listening. I want them to know that they came from a woman who chose love every single day, even when it was hard.

And maybe, one day, when they are chasing dreams of their own, they'll feel what I often feel when I'm lost: that soft whisper from above, from the man who gave me my stubborn fire. *"You've got this."*

Because I do.

And because I'm not done yet.

Archita Singh
@banarasbyarchita

CARMEN AMRIT

"Let 'La Loca' lead the way home."

The wind howled that morning, but it wasn't the cold that made me shake. They were carrying him wrapped in deerskin. His body limp, his spirit gone.

They sang a song of mourning, a cruel melody that would haunt my bones long after my voice had vanished.

I knew before they arrived. The moment the men returned without him, I knew. My knees hit the ground. Something inside me split open.

I screamed with no words, a guttural sound, raw, animal, ancient. I bit down hard enough to taste blood. I didn't want to scream. I didn't want to fall apart. But it was too late. The scream tore from me like a creature giving birth to its own death.

He had promised me forever. And forever lasted only until the claws of the beast found his chest. The women tried to hold me, but I was unreachable. They said nothing. There were no words for this rupture.

I lost my voice that night. Maybe as a punishment. Or maybe it was for protection.

I howled like a wolf. I howled the pain. For days. For lifetimes. Not just silence – absence. A hollowing.

My voice came back, but I wasn't able to articulate any words. I forgot the taste of food. Breathing felt like swallowing knives. And then, the nausea. The sign. The quiet swell in my belly that wasn't grief. It was life. His child.

I said nothing. In this life, I would carry silence too, for other reasons.

In the tribe, they would have seen it as sacred. The child of a fallen warrior and a future shaman. But I couldn't carry his memory inside me. Not after the betrayal. Not after the promise broken by death. It wasn't vengeance, it was survival.

To forget. To bury him with everything. It wasn't revenge. It was unbearable love. I couldn't live without him. So I went to the river. Alone. With herbs, and silence. I bled under the moonlight. And no one ever knew.

Centuries later, I stood shaking in a quiet room in Barcelona, the city I now called home. I was born in Manresa, a city just sixty kilometers away, but I never felt I truly belonged there. I always imagined I'd live in Barcelona, though I didn't know when or how. After two years in New York City, I returned to Spain in 2001, and then, almost effortlessly, found myself moving to Barcelona.

There I was in 2021, with incense curling in the corners and tissues in my hand, a woman across from me whispered gently, "Trust what your body remembers." Then I broke. Sobs that made no sense. Tears that didn't belong to this life. My rational mind tried to grab the wheel, but my body, my body was back at the river.

I saw her – the woman I once was. She was crying, asking for forgiveness, and sobbing in front of the love of her life asking to forgive her for having lost the baby.

And I, this modern, business-building, sperm-donor-choosing woman, was the one doing the crying. But in my mind's eye, I was seeing her, the woman from another lifetime, kneeling by the river, begging for forgiveness from the man she had lost. What the f*ck?

I don't know if it was an actual past life, a vision, a dream, or just a deep emotional metaphor breaking through the noise. But it cracked something open, and I couldn't ignore it.

I was there. Fully. Grieving. Apologising. Shaking. And strangely, something shifted. Not because the past was fixed, but because I finally stopped hiding it from myself.

The truth is, I thought I was asking him for forgiveness. But the real deal? I was asking for my own.

It wasn't until years later that I understood the weight I was carrying was mine, not his. Not all of it. But enough to keep me stuck.

It took me three years of motherhood, of grief, of trying to get it all 'right', to finally get it. That was the real initiation.

Although now I see... the journey had started long before. About a decade earlier, I was watching *Lipstick Jungle* when one of the characters froze her eggs. I had never considered that option before, but something clicked. *"Maybe that's what I'll do,"* I thought. *"Maybe that'll buy me time to figure out if I want to be a mom on my own, or wait and see if someone comes into my life."*

So I did it. I froze my eggs, thinking it was just a temporary pause. Ten years passed. The eggs stayed frozen. The man never came.

And yet, the whisper of motherhood never left. Even two years before I finally made the decision, I had a baby girl's name in my mind. I was happy in many ways. Content. But the longing was still there. And I'd learned to follow my intuition, especially when it refuses to quiet down.

So I said yes. I defrosted the eggs – not many, but just enough. One embryo. One transfer. One heartbeat. The ride of motherhood began.

By then, my body had already crossed a threshold. It was pregnant – full of life, full of hormones, full of things I couldn't control. Once you've crossed that threshold, nothing stays the same.

And honestly? I was naive. I truly believed that all the therapy, all the coaching, all the self-development I had done before would somehow save me from the fall. But, it didn't. And just to make things more 'fun', I decided it was the perfect time to start a business. Yes. That kind of 'crazy'. Years earlier, I had flirted with the idea...

In the early days, I was like a curious bystander, quietly eavesdropping on this new digital world, women talking about lead magnets, newsletters, personal brands. I watched from the sidelines. At first, I told myself it was because I needed to learn. And that was partly true. But deeper down... that answer smelled like a survival mechanism.

The truth? I was struggling with what abundance really meant – not in theory, but in my bones. After becoming a mother, everything shifted. I wanted to create something of my own. I wanted more space, more presence, more purpose. And still, something in me hesitated. Starting a business? It felt wildly unsafe. Because abundance wasn't just about money, it was about visibility. Trusting myself. Expansion. And none of that was familiar territory.

When something isn't familiar, the brain throws up red flags. It's wired to keep you safe, not successful. So when you step too far outside the 'safe zone', it doesn't throw a party. It activates the survival system. That's why we often feel resistance when we try something new – not because we're broken or unprepared, but because the brain has to work harder to process the unfamiliar.

It thinks: New = unsafe. Whether the fear comes from your own life, a past life, or a memory passed down through your lineage, it doesn't really matter. The response is the same: stay small, stay quiet, stay safe.

The thing is... I wasn't alone anymore. My daughter was here. And with her, the voice of truth. She wasn't going to believe what I said. She was going to absorb who I was. And that terrified me. And moved me. So I did it. I started with my typical attitude: "Okay. I have no clue what the hell I'm doing. But I'm following the clues."

And then... something else cracked open: not just a new business, a new definition of abundance. Because suddenly, it wasn't just about strategy, clients, or income goals. It wasn't even about business. It was deeper. Older. Woven into my very foundations.

Right around that time, we were finishing the renovation of two rooms in my grandparents' house, the oldest part of it. The part where my great-great-grandmother once lived. Where my great-grandmother was born. Where my grandfather had to hide during the war. It felt symbolic. Like we were clearing history. Resetting something.

There I was, sprinting from one task to another – unpacking boxes, figuring out how the new induction stove worked, while someone shouted from the hallway, "How do you fix this thing?" My phone buzzed. The cleaning robot got stuck under the sofa – again. Someone needed help with the oven. My daughter tugged at my leg – "Mama, I need to pee!" Every string in the house had come alive and was pulling me in a different direction. One to the kitchen. One to the bathroom. One to the mattress delivery. One to my inbox, my unfinished task list, my unread messages.

Was this just house chaos? Or a glimpse into the kind of the life I was unconsciously building? Because here I was, starting a business. Mothering a toddler. Holding on to a 'stable job'. Trying to meditate, journal, be present, text my friends back. And somewhere in there, talk about abundance? Who was I kidding? I was drowning in logistics, adrenaline, and anxiety, talking about abundance while embodying scarcity. Scarcity of time. Energy. Attention. Breath. I knew something had to change.

Yes, I wanted to build a business. Yes, I wanted to be a present mother. But I didn't want to fall into the trap. The hustle. The guilt. The invisible hamster wheel that swallows your joy and spits out burnout. Where you end up missing time with your kids, blaming everything at once.

And one day, by a lake, while my daughter played nearby and the breeze finally quieted the noise in my head... I asked myself: *Is this what I mean by abundance?* Because if this is what it looks like... it doesn't feel abundant at all.

That's when I knew – I didn't need more theory. I needed embodiment. I needed to live my definition of abundance, not just talk about it. I call it "bringing it down." From the head to the heart. From the concept to the cells.

I started to put words to something I had never fully questioned: *What does abundance truly mean for me?* Because how could I call myself abundant when I was micromanaging every detail, clenched with anxiety, constantly chasing and never arriving? Losing the moment of joy with my daughter and the vision of the precious nature of the lake.

I realised that self-worth is the seed of abundance, and I couldn't receive what I didn't believe I deserved. I had to stop shrinking, stop apologising, and stop negotiating with my own value.

I realised that abundance wasn't about doing more, it was about being more. When I stopped pushing, let go of control, and trusted my intuition, life began to flow in ways I never could have predicted.

I realised that the foundation of manifestation was internal connection. When I stopped abandoning myself and started listening to my body, my nervous system became my ally, not my enemy.

I realised that the beliefs I carried weren't just mine, they were inherited. But the healing? That, I chose. And that choice rippled across generations.

And most of all, I realised that surrender is a kind of strength. My daughter taught me that. Watching her play without planning, live without fear of being too much – that's the kind of freedom I was reclaiming.

So from that place, this is what I now stand for in my work and life: Not perfection. Not productivity. Not performance.

But truth. Power. Presence.

My work empowers women entrepreneurs and leaders to boldly reclaim their voice, own their power, and step into abundant living, all without sacrificing their true selves. I guide this transformation through a powerful blend of Rapid Transformational Therapy (hypnotherapy), Cognitive Metaprogramming, and Kundalini Activation, weaving together intuition, strategy, and embodied energy to unlock their fullest potential.

I'm not here to teach women how to be more efficient. I'm here to remind them they don't have to tame themselves to belong. That their wildness, their vision, and their intuition are not liabilities – they are sacred fires meant to guide their way.

This is my quiet revolution, based on what I now know deep in my bones:

- I don't want to be a good student of the system;
- I don't want women to burn out proving their worth;
- I don't want us to dim our light just to be liked;
- I don't want success to cost us our joy, our softness, or our soul;
- I don't want another woman to hide her brilliance to make others feel comfortable.

I want a world where our bodies, our voices, our desires, and our dreams are not something we apologise for. Where we can mother, create, and lead from the same place: truth.

That is the essence of my journey.

That is what it has meant for me to become a mother and to be a businesswoman.

That is what happens when we stop pretending – and finally let *La Loca* (our wildest and most true part of ourselves) lead the way home.

Carmen Amrit
@carmenamrit
www.carmenamrit.com

KARINA JACKSON

"How do you turn something you love into something that matters to others?"

When I left Paris, I had no idea that one day I would be taking over a non-profit association as President, sewing for a cause, finding my passion in volunteering, and wanting to create my own non-profit association. It is through experiences, opportunities, and connections that I found my purpose and my passion.

I arrived in Barcelona with my husband and my son in August, 2012. We had an apartment, my husband had a job, and my son had a school. Little did I know that I would be offered a job at the same school, just two days before the school year started, as a part-time French teacher.

One doesn't end up in a new city by chance. Barcelona opened up to me, and I have found my true self in this amazing city. This is why I have a *panot* tattooed on my left upper arm. A *panot* is a small, square cement tile with a four-petal flower engraved on it. They can be seen on the pavements in Barcelona. It is an emblematic symbol of the city, and such a simple design, so it felt natural for me to have it as a tattoo to represent my love and gratitude for this beloved city.

In 2015, I started working as the International Baccalaureate Creativity Activity Service (IB CAS) coordinator at Benjamin Franklin International School. This position opened doors to me. The CAS programme is part of the IB diploma where students take on creativity, activity, and service experiences outside the classroom. It allows them to be challenged, step outside their comfort zone, and develop or improve new skills they don't learn at school. I started volunteering when I took on this position because I felt that I had to be a role model for the students, someone to entice the students to do service as part of their IB CAS programme.

Through volunteering with my students, I discovered a new side to them, which is so important to see. Many of them have thanked me for helping them discover how much it means to help people who have been marginalised by society. Also, volunteering made me so curious to learn more. I read books and watched films and documentaries about refugees, invited refugees to the school, and connected with them afterwards so I could learn more about their stories and struggles.

My yoga teacher told me about Esperança and their work with the homeless. The first time I volunteered for them, I made soup that was taken around to feed the homeless by volunteers called 'walkers'. I remember taking in the scene as volunteers were talking and getting the food ready for the trolleys. I didn't do the walk myself. Why? To be honest, I was quite apprehensive. I had never interacted with the homeless before. I didn't know what to expect, what to say, or what I might be exposed to. I was also afraid of how I would react when faced with the reality of how they were living.

Soon, I decided it was time to step outside my comfort zone and be a walker. On Saturday, 26th of November, 2016, I did my first Esperança walk – the Poble Sec and Raval route. Along with a Russian volunteer, also a first-timer, and an English lady who was a regular volunteer, we distributed food and clothes to the homeless. Some of the homeless were sleeping on benches, others had built their own little shelters with blankets and cardboard boxes, while some lay on old mattresses they'd found on the streets. They carried their belongings, well, what little they had, in a suitcase or a backpack. Some of the young Sub-Saharan African men would gather together with their trolleys, often filled with metal they'd collected that day, ready to sell the next morning.

It is one thing seeing people sleeping rough on the streets when you pass by them, but actually giving them food and connecting with them was something else. It is hard to put words into this feeling. It is so humbling, overwhelming, and powerful. I have a lot of respect for the homeless and have a lot of time for them. Before the walk, I would judge them. But who am I to judge someone whose story I don't know? How and why they ended up in the streets is none of our business. The homeless have been ignored for so long, looked down on, spat at, kicked... But they are humans. The only thing that separates us from them is luck and privilege.

Volunteering, seeing the reality that the homeless have to go through every single day and hearing stories from refugees and asylum seekers, really had an impact on how I feel and see the world. A guilt about my privilege opened. I felt the need to help people, provide basic needs, and give my time to those who have been excluded from mainstream society.

When I chat and check in with the homeless people we support, I never ask about their stories, as it is a very personal question that could spark resentment or revive past trauma. But sometimes they offer to share their stories. I remember an Algerian man in his mid-thirties who was sleeping rough by a bank in Poble Sec. I asked his name, and he went on to talk about why he had ended up in Spain on the streets. It broke my heart when he said that back home his wife and young son had died in a car accident. He just couldn't stay and felt the need to run away from his life. No, he didn't end up on the streets because of addiction (which is often the reason people think someone becomes homeless), but because of a terrible loss.

According to the Arrels Foundation, there were 1,231 people sleeping on the streets in Barcelona in 2023. I honestly don't know how they manage to survive out there, year after year. It's tough. I specifically remember this Italian who had arrived in Barcelona only a few days before, looking for a friend but with no idea where he was staying. He was sleeping rough with another friend in Poble Sec. I regularly saw him on the walks and was shocked by how he changed. His skin looked rough and he was clearly addicted, something he may not have been prior to becoming homeless.

One evening in November 2024, a homeless man asked if he could come to the Esperança premises to get some food. Little did I know that he would become a dear friend and one of the success stories from the homeless community. We had communicated before, but when he walked in that Saturday evening, we hugged straight away. From Iran, he spoke English and had the kindest face. There was a gentleness about him, in his voice and his manner, and he carried himself with quiet dignity. Back in Iran, he had earned a university degree, worked full-time, and travelled widely. Yet because of who he loved, he was no longer safe. He faced the constant risk of jail, lashes, or even the death penalty under Iran's laws. His family helped him escape after the authorities discovered his homosexuality, but the cost was leaving everything behind and starting again, alone, in a new country.

When he arrived in Barcelona, he had no legal papers and was forced to live on the streets. He would come to the Esperança premises for food and clothes, and even began volunteering with us. When he was able to get support from Acathi, a local association that supports LGBTQ+ refugees and asylum seekers, slowly things changed. He eventually obtained the right to live and work here, found a job, and now has a place to sleep. He is an amazing, smart, resilient, and optimistic person, one of the kindest people I know. His journey is proof that homelessness has many faces. As a former homeless person, now turned comedian and friend, Iain Anderson, once said: *"Love other people like their lives depend on it."*

Now I am proud to help Esperança and other causes in more ways. I am on the board of Esperança, as well as being their school and university partnership coordinator. I also help them with donations through my initiative, *Pelikas – Sewing for a Cause.*

I had always wanted to learn how to sew, and back in 2020, I bought my first sewing machine and booked my first sewing classes. I learned the very basics in a three-day workshop where I learned to sew a toiletry bag, a cushion cover, and a tote bag. Like a child, I was getting excited and practised making those accessories. I started watching tutorials on YouTube, and I began sewing reversible tote bags, some simple zipped pouches, as well as some bookmarks. I posted my creations on Facebook to show what I did.

A colleague reached out to me and said, "Why don't you sell your handmade items at our Christmas craft fair?" Of course I said yes, and the funds were donated to Esperança. I started sewing more, taking orders after the fair. I was thrilled to say the least. I was mainly selling to my colleagues, and because it was during the COVID pandemic, I made a lot of facemasks. One day, I decided to give a name to my social sewing project and decided on *Pelikas*. I created an Instagram page, and also designed a logo with the 'K' as open scissors.

Now I create accessories with a double purpose: the buyer has a beautiful, handmade accessory, while donating to help those in need. I sell to friends, Mamas in Biz members, Esperança volunteers, and also via Etsy and Instagram. Sewing takes a lot of time, it isn't just about the stitches; it's choosing fabric, cutting, ironing, pinning, unpinning, sewing, unpicking, and starting again. The sewing itself is the easy part, it's all the work around it that makes every accessory truly unique. The purchaser pays me for the cost of the fabric, and the rest of the proceeds go directly to charities such as Esperança and Acathi.

I also support the LGBTQ+ community, refugees, and asylum seekers. The LGBTQ+ community is another part of society that is often targeted, and in over sixty-four countries, because of their sexuality or their gender (especially for transgender individuals), they can be imprisoned or executed. Like everyone else, they deserve to be safe, to live openly, to be loved, and have access to the same support the rest of us do.

I have also always dreamed about creating my own non-profit association. This project has been growing slowly in my head. My idea is to open a social café in Barcelona. A safe place where people from the marginalised community could come for a hot drink or a snack, connect with neighbours, share stories, and exchange services. An Iranian asylum seeker could teach maths to a single mum's young boy, and in return, she might cook him a meal or help him learn Catalan. An elderly man could teach a young refugee to read, and the young man could fix the elderly man's bike. The possibilities are endless.

The idea is that one day it could become a cooperative, creating jobs for the people who use the café and its services. *You give something, we give you something.* It's about creating jobs, giving people a purpose, helping them learn new skills, and offering them love and attention.

Why do we so often forget that what people need is to feel a part of something? We need to be cared for, to be supported, and to have a reason to get up in the morning.

Through this journey of giving back, I have found my passion for sewing and volunteering, my *raison d'être*. And it's not just sewing, but 'sewing for a cause'.

Karina Jackson Lorenzo
@pelikascostura
@esperancabcn
www.esperancabarcelona.com

JIMENA GUISLAIN

"I don't want other single mothers to live this alone."

I arrived in Madrid from Peru in 2006 when I was almost twenty years old. I lived the most incredible thirteen years there: I became an adult, fell in love, got my heart broken, and learned to rebuild myself. I learned how to stand on my own. I also learned to fall down and get back up again.

Madrid was my home, my emotional school, and also my first real mirror. It showed me everything I could be... and everything I was not yet. But there came a time when it was no longer enough for me. After so many years, something broke. Or maybe it was me who broke.

A relationship that promised to be forever ended a month before the '*I do*', and with it fell the whole structure I had built in my head. When that relationship ended, everything I thought was stable – partner, home, future – fell apart. Madrid was no longer mine.

I left. Not as one who flees, but as one who says goodbye to a stage that no longer fits.

I arrived in Barcelona with doubts. It wasn't like Madrid. It wasn't like anything. And I was working too hard and earning too little.

I had to become a fan of myself, because there was no one to pass the shift to. Between tears, resumes, and dinners on European schedules, I was rebuilding myself.

I don't know if I was reborn... but at least I didn't become extinct. And that, sometimes, is enough.

Eventually, I met a group of Argentines who made me feel that maybe everything could get better. I met them through Bumble BFF – *obvioooo.* I went back to laughing, hanging out, talking until late like I was twenty again. It was with that group that I met a guy, Anton, who eventually became the father of my daughter.

In 2022, I was living with Anton and became unemployed. My relationship with Anton was falling apart, but I kept trying. I thought about separating, but with no job, I felt more secure staying with him. But I wasn't happy, and I couldn't find a job...

Something had to change! And it did change... I decided to get a master's degree.

I thought maybe focusing on getting a degree in something I'm passionate about (digital marketing) would make finding a job easier, and then I would be able to make a decision about my relationship and future with Anton.

I enrolled with fear but also a lot of hope. I was doing this for me. And just when I thought I only needed to recharge my professional life, surprise: I was pregnant.

I felt an unexpected happiness. But the day I told Anton I was pregnant, he left me... I was only six weeks pregnant.

That day, he didn't just leave me. That day he made it clear to me that I was going to write this story on my own. I suffered a hurt that one should not suffer, and I cried non-stop. And on top of that, I was already starting to feel the famous maternal guilt: for not feeding myself well, for not walking enough, for not doing prenatal yoga or singing songs... I worried I would not be able to give my baby the life I had as a child. And it pained me to think that what I was capable of giving was not enough.

Eventually, I got a job and moved back to the apartment where I lived before I met Anton. Going back there was like finding an old version of me, but this time with a belly. And finally, that day I stopped crying. I felt something like peace. Things were starting, very slowly, to fall into place. I worked during the day, studied for my master's degree in the afternoon-evening, and survived as best I could in that Barcelona summer – an intense heat that was cooking me from the inside.

The end of the pregnancy was a mix of fear, exhaustion, and small personal victories, like putting the baby's room together by myself, with my belly getting in the way and the YouTube tutorial paused every three minutes. No one helped me. But that room turned out beautifully. It was my way of telling her, *"I'm waiting for you, even if I'm exhausted, even if I'm alone."*

The delivery was an emergency C-section. And yes, it was scary, but I still remember it with a smile. I was strong and I responded well. The next day, I was walking around as if I hadn't been cut open. I was exhausted, but I had my daughter. For a moment, it all made sense.

That moment was brief.

Reality hit: failed breastfeeding, no sleep, and my master's breathing down my neck. I was broken, literally in pieces.

My mother travelled all the way from Peru to help me. She was seventy-three years old, had a sore spine, and a list of unsolicited advice. I hated her a little too. Sometimes I felt like I had two babies to take care of. But she loved Valentina from minute zero, and that is something I will never forget.

I did it as well as I could. I did it the messy, real way. Like a real woman, dishevelled, emotionally collapsed, and wanting to sleep for three years in a row...

Breastfeeding (or rather, its absence) was a blow. One early morning I ended up in the emergency room because I couldn't stop crying. I was told that there was no psychologist on call. I was told to come back on Monday. They sent me home.

That's when I hit bottom. That's when I let go. I let go of the guilt. I let go of the pressure. I let go of the need to meet other people's standards. And there – right there – I felt reborn.

Being reborn hurts because it breaks you before it rebuilds you. It's not smooth. It's not immediate. To be reborn is to let go of versions of yourself that you thought were permanent. It is about accepting that plans are not going to happen the way you dreamed. It is being alone while everything changes. It is learning without anyone teaching you. It is to look at yourself in the mirror without recognising yourself... and to go on.

But it is also the only real way to return to meaningful living.

Maternity leave ended in what seemed like the blink of an eye. Valentina was only three months old when I left her for the first time at daycare. Three months... I wasn't ready to go back to work. I thought she wouldn't be ready to be left alone with people she didn't know either.

I went back to work in pieces, with my head trapped between mental lists: paediatrician, vaccines, milk, diapers, medical appointments, nap schedules, unanswered emails, pending master's degree assignments. All mixed up, all at the same time, and all sleeping badly.

Still, I gave it everything I could. I wanted to prove – and prove to myself – that I could do this too. That being a mother didn't *cancel me out* as a professional. Spoiler: yes, you can do it all... but not all at the same time, and not without consequences.

At work, I had exactly the same targets as my peers. No adjustments, no "how are you?" and no "do you need anything?" Just numbers. And even though I tried to reach them, the truth is, I couldn't.

One day I received a formal email with copies to all my bosses giving me an official warning: "We want to give you a wake-up call because you are not hitting targets."

Meanwhile, the master's program continued. I still had to present the last projects, finalise the coursework, and prepare for graduation.

I collapsed – between crying helplessly and feeling the sheer lack of empathy. After all that, and after an anxiety crisis that left me trembling in the bathroom, I accepted what I had been denying for months: anxiety leave.

Graduation ceremony day arrived. The graduation that I had dreamed of throughout my pregnancy as the day when I would finally celebrate. A closing. A victory. A respite. This day was to be the celebration of EVERYTHING I had been able to accomplish alone. All the efforts, the tears, the struggles. I dreamed of the photo I would have with my diploma and my baby in my arms. A photo that I would proudly hang in my little girl's room so she would know that her mother was a fighter and that I had done everything for her. I had completed a master's degree, whole and broken at the same time: sleep deprived, with a newborn baby, my body open and my mind overloaded. But I had done it. I was so proud...

When I arrived at the graduation ceremony at the Palau Sant Jordi, with my daughter in my arms, the first thing I heard was: "You can't go in with the child."

There was no alternative and no understanding. Just a door closed in my face.

I wasn't allowed in with my baby. They told me to leave her with strangers. I refused and was in tears. That day I understood: not even in the celebration of my own achievements was there room for me, a single mother. I sat outside, waiting for my guests to leave the premises.

I wept uncontrollably. Not only because of what I was being denied, but because of what it meant. I did not attend my graduation that day, but that day I understood something that marked me forever: I don't want other mothers to live this alone.

If no one opens space for us, then we have to build it. Between the pain, the rage, and a baby sleeping on me, *Single Moms BCN* was born.A community created from exclusion, but with the strength of not wanting to be left out anymore.

After the 'no graduation ceremony' I made a video on my personal social networks explaining what had happened, and little by little it reached many people. Mothers (not necessarily single) who were as outraged as I was.

Suddenly, I got a call from *La Vanguardia* newspaper who wanted to interview me. I was freaking out. But yes, yes, and yes! Let this transcend! Let it be known, let us have visibility.

I was also contacted by RTVE, who invited me to give an interview on the set. And so it was.

Single Moms BCN began, not as a brand strategy, nor as a well thought out project. It was born out of necessity. From that feeling of always being on the tightrope and having no one below in case you fall.

The idea of *Single Moms BCN* was to create a community. A place where motherhood means belonging, not exclusion. I didn't want what happened to me during my pregnancy and postpartum to happen to anyone else.

Because every mommy needs a tribe. A helping hand. A listening ear.

I created a WhatsApp group and an Instagram account, and organised the first event with fear, doubts, babies in tow, and emotional backpacks heavier than strollers. But they came, and we laughed and we hugged without knowing each other.

Today *Single Moms BCN* is not only a social space. It is also a way to say, *"Here we are,"* in a world that makes us invisible.

In the Whatsapp group I organise events, yes, but we also create a network, containment, and visibility. Because there is no public policy that contemplates us, and without community, it becomes unbearable.

I want to invite you to stay connected. Because *Single Moms BCN* doesn't end with a book or a post. It's a community on the move. A project that grows. A space under permanent construction, like us.

Jimena Guislain
@singlemomsbcn
www.singlemomsbcn.com

AMANDA O'SHEA

"What if we are always connected to our inner wisdom?"

Every tale has a beginning. I was born happy in the summer of 1969, in Maida Vale, West London. Gifted with a stable childhood, and enjoying a wild lust for life and travel since I was a young girl, I have always felt a hippie at heart, and a fairy at play. A gap year in the 1980s turned into a colourful decade of adventure around the world.

I had a swift return back to London in 1996 from Hong Kong, after I fell pregnant with my firstborn, a beautiful boy named Charlie. My lovely daughter Alice was born a couple of years later, and even though I fully adored pregnancy and motherhood, it wasn't easy for me to settle back in the UK. There were more than enough bumps in the road; I witnessed unhealthy habits around me, life wasn't the family fairytale my head had romanticised, and a separation from the children's father was inevitable. My heart knew there was a different life out there; I'd lived that life, the free spirit of adventure, embraced by blue skies, sea, and sunshine. The pull for change was strong.

A few people I knew had made the move to Spain, and when I visited them, I never wanted to return home. Charlie had just turned ten, and Alice was seven. After a couple of 'reccy' trips to look at schools, 'The Three Amigos' were off, in our new red and white kombi campervan, which had always been on my bucket list!

I remember having to tell my wonderful family and friends that I was leaving the UK. Again. Some shook their heads and asked me, "Do you even know where you're going?" I knew I was heading south. I had rented an apartment in a beautiful town called Jávea, in the pearl of the Costa Blanca. But I didn't know the language yet.

Quickly, we set roots, welcomed two dogs into our Spanish home, and started living the dream. We had a good life, my heart sang from the inside out. I opened a home clinic with the skills I brought with me as a holistic therapist. I chose hours that suited our family, as best I could as a single mum. It wasn't all plain sailing, but we bobbed along. The children also found and followed their paths.

Connection after connection paved my way; my holistic work led me into resilience coaching. The years of extended professional training to become a Three Principles Coach changed my world. I deepened my understanding of the inside-out creation of reality, discovering peace of mind.

Speaking at a wellbeing event led to me being offered my own radio show. *Happy Hour with Amanda* went 'live on-air'! A few years later, a radio listener introduced me to a new, exclusive addiction treatment centre in town. And so it is... one thing always leading to the next.

One morning in February 2017, I woke up excited. A new client had just signed up for my coaching course, 'The Serendipity Experience.' It was Day 1 of our initial three-day deep dive. We had plans to climb El Montgó, our local mountain. The first session is always memorable, as we 'walk & talk' to connect. The client opens up, and a few seeds are sown, as we stroll in silence, allowing space for their mind to settle and insights to bubble up. All in the awe and wonder of a day in nature, the strength of the mountain was ready to hug us.

The weather had been a little 'iffy', but it can change in a heartbeat. I prayed for no rain. A phone call from the new recovery centre (where I'd been hoping to get my foot in the door) disrupted my flow. I noticed the time and felt the pressure of being late; there was no chance for a proper dog walk before heading out. Usually, I would never bring the dogs on a first session with a client. But then, clear as a bell, came the whisper from within: *Take them with you. Don't even ask.*

When my client arrived, I said with my fingers crossed, "I thought it would be nice to bring the dogs if that suits you."

She smiled as she said, "Sure, I love dogs."

Thank God for that. And off we went.

We began our climb, and the dogs were in their element, but the mountain felt damp, the clouds were low, and again, I felt that same inner guidance: *Turn around. It's not safe to climb high today.* Without hesitation, I suggested, "Shall we head back and continue the session at Casa Serendipity?" She agreed.

What I didn't expect was to return home and find smoke. I couldn't process it fully at first, but then, I had the awful realisation: my house was on fire.

I put the dogs back in the campervan and called emergency services. It felt like a long wait until I heard the sirens in the distance, coming across the valley from Dénia fire station. I stood watching, strangely calm, while neighbours gathered. The black smoke thickened and oozed from the windows.

People looked at me, some with worry, some with curiosity. But again, I heard the whisper: *Everything is going to be okay.*

I turned to check on my client, she looked shell-shocked. I tried to lighten the moment: "Talk about coaching in action." She didn't find it funny. Fair enough.

The deeper truth settled in. *If I hadn't brought the dogs with me today...* It doesn't bear thinking about. What if I had ignored my intuition? This story could have ended very differently. I now prayed for the rain, the polar opposite of that morning's wishes.

I didn't know what had started the fire. My mind darted through the house: the Himalayan salt lamp, the spare phone on charge, the radiator... had I left porridge on the stove? No, the smoke was pouring from my treatment room.

Once the fire was under control, I was given a hard hat and allowed briefly to enter the ground floor with a fireman. The roof had partially collapsed. Everything was black. Charred. Gone. The smell was stifling. What a mess! A flash of colour caught my eye amidst the charred remains, I spotted remnants of my favourite raspberry red raincoat, bought in West Cork, reduced to a scrap. That hit unexpectedly hard. There did not appear to be anything to salvage.

The house was being boarded up and locked for inspection as my neighbour Karen appeared. She smiled warmly as she handed me her house keys on her way back to work, "I've just heard, I'm so sorry. Move into mine and help yourself to anything. No better woman to deal with this than you, Amanda."

As I stepped out of the shower at Karen's place, looking at my stinky clothes in a bin bag, it hit me: *I didn't even own a pair of knickers anymore!* Everything had gone. And yet, what remained was profound.

I don't dwell on the fire often. However, when I reflect on the pivotal moments of my life, that day stands out. Not because of the loss of material things, but because my inner voice spoke, and I listened. That inner whisper I had spent years learning to trust was clearer than ever. And I acted on it, without doubt or hesitation.

A friend was worried, "You can't be alright, you just lost your home and everything you own." But I was alright, and it is strangely comforting to lose it all, and yet know you really are okay.

That day, everything I had ever learned, practised, and taught about intuition, wisdom, and presence was real and embodied. It wasn't just theory; it was resilience in action. I remain forever thankful that we were all safe.

We never know what's around the corner, but I take great comfort in truly knowing that I already have whatever I need inside of me to navigate life and any turbulent times. I have had my share of chaotic moments, like most people, but I always seem to land on my feet. The day after the fire, the Head of Clinic at the recovery centre resigned, and I was offered the job, including a villa with a pool, and all expenses paid. You can't make it up!

The experience and growth that I gained during my years working at that recovery centre have had the most significant impact on my work as a resilience coach. Working with people at the height of their anxiety and full-blown addictions inspired me to shift and collaborate on a project for teenagers and families. Holding hope in the light of prevention and mental health education, I launched 'Resilient Living' and 'iheart' programmes in Spain.

In lockdown 2020, a contact from the radio invited me to officiate a funeral. A young man had taken his own life, and the family asked me to celebrate his being. It wasn't an easy gig for my first ceremony. Ironically, somebody there said, "You should also be doing weddings."

Before long, I had trained with The Academy of Modern Celebrancy, and my wedding bookings brought me up to Catalunya. I fell in love with Barcelona and relocated. Again. This time, just me and the iconic kombi campervan. My children were grown up and settled; the dogs had passed away peacefully from old age. I started hosting a clinic in the heart of Barcelona, offering my holistic services and resilience coaching for adults and adolescents, and I even started singing with 250 people in the Barcelona English Choir!

The connections I've made along the way have served me well. As one introduction led to the next opportunity, with a sunny disposition and a sprinkle of 'let's give it a go!', my story has unfolded, and whispers of wisdom continue to guide me. It's been hypnotising and mesmerising; plenty of fun days, a few lonely nights, highs, lows, surprises, unexpected challenges, the full shebang.

It's not until after the dust settles that we pause to reflect... insights occur, and we join up the dots. Our 'thought system' is innocently creating our reality, moment to moment, whether we realise that or not; the good, the bad, and the ugly, and consciousness brings it all alive! It feels so real - it's meant to!

Everything I have ever designed is with the premise to guide my clients back to who they are at their core. We explore together to deepen their understanding of how the mind works, to 'unlearn' and bust myths that are not serving them well. To embrace life with less stress and more joy, as we slow down to the speed of love.

Being self-employed in Spain has never been very easy from a bureaucratic standpoint, and I wouldn't describe working in the recovery field as a breeze. Nevertheless, one thing is certain: none of it has been boring, and there is so much learning in times of discomfort. I see LIFE as my soulmate, and hold no regrets about taking each leap of faith and following its nudges.

A new client asked me a great question:

"Amanda, how do you define resilience?"

I answered: "What if resilience is knowing, beyond a shadow of a doubt, that your wellbeing is innate, and not conditional upon anyone or anything. Nothing is missing, lacking, or broken, just hidden waiting to be unveiled and activated."

The moon waxes and wanes, and waxes again... There is spring, summer, autumn, winter, and then the spring returns...

Amanda O'Shea
@amandaoshea.coach
@yourlovinglifecelebrant
www.amandaoshea.com

PAULA ECHEVERRI

"Being authentic means showing up as your real self – not the version you think you should be."

I never thought that silence could be a gift. I never imagined that losing something so essential like my hearing could actually lead me to something even more powerful: finding myself.

For years, I lived in a world filled with sound, conversations, and noise. I was living a very fast-paced life with my own business, working with tech companies in the San Francisco Bay Area. Originally from Colombia, my parents moved to California when I was a young child. I had what many would call a perfect life with my husband and two girls. But sometimes, when you are used to being in the hustle and bustle, you think a busy life is normal. The reality was, I was not taking care of myself or my spiritual life at all, which I now realise was something I needed badly.

When you least expect it, life gives you a STOP sign and makes you reflect. And one day, my world changed. After I gave birth to my second daughter in 2013, my hearing started to fade, and I was left with something I had never experienced before – silence. It was terrifying. I felt disconnected, isolated, and even lost. I had to reinvent the way I communicated, the way I worked, and the way I lived.

At first, I fought the silence. I tried to hold on to the life I knew, to force my way back into the world of sound. But no matter how hard I tried, the silence remained.

I saw numerous doctors with no answers, healers, acupuncturists, therapists... I tried everything I could to find out why this happened, but I never found out.

I had severe anxiety, stress, and panic attacks, and I had no idea how to manage my emotions. This instilled in me a desire to start learning what was happening to me and my body. I started to research and learnt that emotions affect the whole mind and body. I went back to college to study neuroscience.

I started to finally understand what was going on in my mind, and then, something shifted. I stopped fighting it. I started listening – not to the outside world, but to myself. To my beautiful mess... For the first time, I could truly hear my own thoughts, my intuition, my inner wisdom. The silence became my teacher and my best friend.

And then in the absence of noise, I found clarity. I started to meditate, something I had never given much thought to before, but had been curious about. I always followed Buddhist teachings. Ever since I was a teenager, I stopped believing in Catholicism, unlike the rest of my family. For some of them, I was a black sheep or the 'weird one'.

When I started meditating, it felt strange, even uncomfortable because I was not used to it. But with time, I realised that meditation wasn't just about relaxation – it was also about transformation and listening to inner wisdom.

As I sat in stillness, my body and mind began to change. Science tells us that meditation can lower stress, improve focus, and even rewire the brain. The most profound shift for me was in how I saw myself.

I had a hearing aid, but most guided meditations did not work for me because the words were often hard to follow. Through a meditation coach, I was introduced to Tibetan bowls. This was a relief, because I could hear the sounds, but I didn't have to concentrate as hard on what was being said. In time, I learnt a lot more about sounds and how they profoundly impact the brain and body. I had this 'aha' moment where everything with the sound meditations started to make sense.

All humans are made of energy and we vibrate at a certain frequency. The sounds were supercharged with frequencies that helped me with many areas of my life that I wanted to work on, like my anxiety and stress. I started using more sound meditations, and I managed to calm my anxiety to the point that it was pretty much gone. It was amazing for me to experience that.

"The human body is a symphony of sounds. Every chakra, every organ, every bone, every tissue, every cell has its own resonant frequency, its own sound. However, when an organ is out of time or out of tune with the rest, then the entire body is affected. This harmony leads to states of disease and disintegration. Frequency plays an important role in identifying the actual problem in the human body."

Amit Sharma and Awadhesh Kumar Maurya: *International Journal of Electrical, Electronics and Data Communication*

I discovered that my brain waves could be changed by using these frequencies. When someone is stressed or anxious, they emit beta waves. So I could change my state to a more beneficial, relaxed mindset in alpha waves, which are better for you during the day and offer an improved emotional outcome.

When I used this, I no longer felt like a victim of my circumstances. I realised that my hearing loss wasn't an end, it was a beginning, a doorway to a deeper connection with myself, and I felt a profound sense of balance in my mind and body.

I did try speech therapy and I had a cochlear implant later on. Four years after my hearing loss, I found myself in a normal place. I had changed in that stillness, I discovered something unexpected: a new version of me. The one lurking in the shadows of my soul... the real me.

In 2020, my husband and I decided to move to Barcelona. I was surrounded by striking architecture and an artistic flair, in comparison to the Bay Area, where everything seemed more black and white and a little grey in between.

Like a chameleon, I felt I was ready to start over with new colours, and the artist in me started to awaken. Ever since I was a small girl, I saw my attorney mum relieve her stress with art.

That urge to make art was a way to purge my deepest emotions and the fear of living in a new country. Now I find my voice in painting or sketching, but it only started when I moved to Spain. The joy in my life is art and being creative, and I find it now a huge key in my process to question why, what is this piece trying to tell me?

During the pandemic, I found out that the marriage to the father of my kids did not make sense anymore. We were not vibrating on the same frequency, as I say now! As I changed and evolved in my journey, we changed, and we could not keep the relationship alive. We both felt we were not the same people we used to be together, and we decided to keep a solid friendship for the benefit of our girls.

I am sure that without all the things that happened to me, I would have reacted in a very different way to the massive amount of changes in my life. But now I feel positive and fulfilled, something that I didn't think would happen. I did the work to get to this point, and it did pay off. Like my twelve-year-old wrote in an essay in school about her parent's divorce, "We are still a team."

Working on my emotional state definitely helped and expanded new, unknown areas in my life, thanks to my research in neuroscience. When you switch the narrative to see things in another light, everything changes. I also learned once and for all to be as authentic as I can for myself and for my girls, as I grow and evolve as a person, a mum, and a human being. Most people don't realise all the masks that we wear every day just for being in a relationship.

I want to be an agent of change for women and their families by speaking about it and never being quiet about what I think that benefits the world. Women's rights are my passion, and I learned in Barcelona to put aside my ego, finally, and be fully who I am unapologetically.

Being authentic means showing up as your real self – not the version you think you 'should' be, but the one that aligns with your values, your emotions, and your truth. It's about parenting with honesty, presence, and self-awareness, even when things become messy or imperfect.

I try to embrace my imperfections every day now. I have limitations: I don't try to be perfect, and that does not stress me anymore. My girls see that, and I hope they can also embrace imperfection. I think that embracing imperfection is key in life to anything you put your mind to.

I love to show my girls my silly side, not just the authoritarian 'Don't do this, Don't do that' mum, but also me as a real person. My girls, for example, had no idea I had a sense of humour. What is she like, really? They had no idea! They only knew the mask of me being a mum, not who I really was. I want my kids to have memories of their silly mum instead of not getting to know me at all! That would be sad, I think.

I also know the value of being in the present moment because the present is a 'gift', as I like to call it. I love to spend time on my own, watching the sunset or just breathing, watching nature and animals. Spain is a beautiful place, and there is so much more to see out there than on my phone screen. I make sure I don't take those moments for granted like I did before, when I was just living and not bringing real joy to my life.

I live my life knowing that the universe always has something better for me, and I see that problems now are not bad things; they are redirections to get to that point in life you need faster.

My mantra:

"Things are always working out for me."

Bryan Hicks

We all experience loss in some way. It might not be our hearing, but maybe it's a job, a relationship, or a version of ourselves that no longer exists. But sometimes, what feels like an ending is really an invitation to something greater.

I definitely feel that losing my hearing made me more attuned to what truly matters. It gave me the courage to step into a new life, to follow my passions, and to help others do the same.

Silence isn't empty, it's full of wisdom. If you take the time to listen, to sit with yourself, and to embrace the stillness, you might just find the answers you've been searching for.

So today, I invite you to pause. To embrace a moment of silence. And to ask yourself: *What is my intuition trying to tell me?* Because in that silence, you might hear the voice that will change your life.

Paula Andrea Echeverri
@themindexplorerceo
www.neuromomceo.com

LOIS IRELAND

"Mine is a butterfly story – a journey from obedient girl to soul-led woman."

In 2016 I was sitting behind a desk, inputting data into a computer. That might be okay for some, but for a creative mind like mine, the monotonous work was beyond draining. The humdrum day-to-day felt heavy, like I was running a marathon in someone else's body. Maybe you know the feeling? My inner critique whispered harsh messages of self-doubt, and sadly squashed my creative self into the shadows. This desperation kept me tethered to the hamster wheel of life, frantically moving but never progressing.

Mine is a butterfly story – a journey from obedient girl to soul-led woman. Let us begin.

From the moment I showed promise with the violin, the direction of my future was set. Being born into a devout Mormon family, which upheld high moral standards and expectations, also predetermined my life. Lois must walk the path of righteousness, marry within the church, and be a violinist. Simple enough, I suppose.

I was a good girl. I did as I was told, and every day I tried to accomplish what was expected of me. I woke up and, without fail, practiced my violin. I performed when requested and played in many different orchestras, some of which I led. The same with church. I attended every Sunday service without question and every activity held at The Mormon Church in York, England. I respectfully took on roles within the church structure and did my best to fulfil them.

Woven into my difficult youth, were happy and fun moments, and I recollect these with fondness. All my friends were within the church. But there was a constant voice in the back of my mind that told me, *"This isn't you."* I was a zombie of 'goodness', living a life that wasn't truly mine.

One day at the age of twenty-three, I chose to finally listen to that voice, and I made the first authentic decision of my life. I left the church! I couldn't stay where I didn't belong. In doing this, I knew the fall out would be intense, and it was brutal. I lost everything and everyone, my whole community shunned me. I was left standing alone, my life shattered around me. I was suddenly isolated, with no idea of the world I had just fumbled into.

I made many mistakes. I hit rock bottom, and it hurt, badly, so why carry on? That was nearly the end of my story. Somehow, I found the inner strength to crawl out from what felt like the never-ending black hole that was my mind. With time and healing, I came to realise that my fractured past didn't own my future and in fact I was now free! Free to do ANYTHING. Free to be ANYONE. I could be ME! But *who was I?*

We are complex creatures, formed of layers. Each layer is created by life experiences and interactions, but at our centre, we have a core self. I came into this world a creator. As a child, my artistic side was appreciated but never realised. BE A VIOLINIST, but I love painting. BE A VIOLINIST, but I love crafting. BE A VIOLINIST, but, but!

These 'buts' were seen as hobbies, nothing of serious consequence. So much time and money had been invested in my violin that it felt selfish to stop. I will pause to show gratitude for my mum. She went through an awful lot in life. She sacrificed so much and worked so hard to give me everything she could, and I love her for it.

I graduated from university (Birmingham Conservatoire) with a BMus (Hons) and found myself overcome by depression. It had crept up slowly and was buried deep into my psyche. It became a cruel companion, speaking through lies and half-truths. Constantly chanting:

"You aren't good enough; you will never be good enough; there are better violinists out there, so why bother."

It chipped away at my confidence and blinded me from the reality that I was a very good violinist.

My violin teacher, Herbert Whone, was inspiring. He was a critical thinker with a fabulous, creative mind. A musician, author, artist, and photographer – a kindred spirit. He had a gentle kindness and showed genuine interest in my artistic skills beyond music, and he encouraged me to pursue them. At the beginning of my violin lessons, he would invite me to critique the painting he was working on. I was ridiculously unqualified, but he never made me feel foolish. A piece of his art hangs in my home, a constant reminder of his kind encouragement.

One day, after what felt like a bad violin performance, I finally gave in to the voice inside me and, with tears in my eyes, I placed my violin under my bed and tried to move forward without it. This was not the best decision, yet oddly, it set my future in motion.

I left home and needed money. I worked two jobs – admin Monday to Friday, and any catering shift I could get during the weekend. I was constantly exhausted. During this time, I kept my creative mind alive. I crafted gifts for friends and family. I made toys and teddies, paintings and intricate 3D art pieces. With time, I tried every artistic expression I knew. That niggling voice still found fault with everything I made, so nothing stuck, yet the smiles that came when receiving my gifts were enough for me to keep trying.

When I wasn't working, I found spiritual respite and mental freedom walking in the country. I felt tiny in the vastness of the Yorkshire countryside. I still have a deep connection to the vibrant green patchwork of the Dales and the mystical purple haze of the heather that haunts the moors. There, my imagination was as wild as the woods and as endless as the sky. Mind you, this natural beauty has the power to ignite and inspire any idle mind.

One fateful Friday, I accepted a late shift at the Jorvik Viking Centre in York. I was to serve wine at a business function there, a function that Andres, a young executive from Barcelona, was attending. He arrived just in time for me to pour him the last glass of wine of my shift. Our eyes met, and the room faded away.

Our souls connected, and we knew we were meant to be together. His passion and conviction were intoxicating; I had never met anyone like him. Two months later, we were engaged, and a year to the day we met, we married! Andres could see through the BS I told myself – he always saw me as an artist, a creator. He gave me the boost to finally leave admin, make amends with my violin, and to study to become a Suzuki violin teacher.

After qualifying, I realised that I truly enjoyed teaching. I taught at the St Albans Music School and within primary schools in Hertfordshire. I started my own home studio, and also set up the St Albans Suzuki baby group, which was so much fun.

In 2018 we were blessed with our first child Elena. Nine months later, in January 2019, we packed up our life in England and moved to Calafell, Spain. Calafell is a small coastal town about an hour south of Barcelona, where Andres' parents live. Their health was a concern at the time and Brexit was imminent, so the move made sense. But for me, it was a difficult decision. With sadness, I said goodbye to my wonderful students, colleagues, friends, and my family, but I stepped into our new life with hope.

Back then my Spanish language skills were basic at best, and Catalan non-existent. This inability to communicate clearly made even the simplest of tasks difficult. I barely left the apartment, with this came social disconnect. Ultimately, it left me lost and lonely. Elena became my world, and I relied on Andres for nearly everything. So, when the pandemic hit, my life barely changed. Except... I started felting! Creating with this new medium came naturally to me. I had finally found *my* artistic expression. I loved the way it felt when handling the wool. The huge array of colours and types of fibre was interesting.

I bought books and watched countless YouTube videos. I started to have fun exploring felting techniques. I learnt how to manipulate the wool with felting needles and water to create anything and everything I could visualise in my mind. Elena would ask me to make her a robin, so I did. A fairy, a mermaid, a butternut squash mouse house (still one of my favourite things I have ever made) with tiny thimble mice, so cute! I felt (pun intended) inspired and happy, more myself than ever.

Soon, I was making felted items and pictures as gifts for friends and family. I received the most wonderful feedback; they hadn't realised that I had made their gifts. My work seemed professional. The joy I saw when people received my felted creations was healing for my soul, a real boost to my spirit.

Soon I was being commissioned to create – a lion, a donkey, more fairies, and wall art. I came to the realisation that I needed to open myself up to being seen. Step out of my comfort zone of only creating for those who know and love me, and offer my art to the world. This terrified me. I was frozen in place once again. I would spend days paralysed on the sofa, freaking out over 'what if' scenarios.

What if I shared my creations and people hated them? What if no one bought them?

Despite this, I continued felting. Soon, I had a small horde of creations hidden in a box. I felt sad for my beautiful things stuck in darkness; it didn't feel right.

Enter Georgina Hudson, a truly marvellous woman. She is empathetic and empowering, with training in Strategic Intervention life coaching, transpersonal psychology, and mindfulness, amongst other things, she gave me the tools to pave my own path. To realise myself professionally and personally.

Who am I? I once asked myself. The answer: I am a creator. I AM A CREATOR! This was difficult to acknowledge for many years, but here I am writing it down for the world to read.

In 2021, Andres and I celebrated the birth of our second daughter Clara. Our precious family was now complete. But little did I know that three years later, I would birth my third creation, my Etsy shop, *Felting Earth by Lois*, where I sell my art, amongst other felted goodies. I had ignited something deep within.

My daughters inspire me daily. They are smart, funny, and very sweet. The way they communicate with each other, when they aren't squabbling, is wonderful. One evening, curled up on the sofa together, Andres and I were chatting about spirit animals for our girls. Both Andres and I simultaneously said Ladybird for Elena, and then an image of a bright blue dragonfly appeared in my mind's eye for Clara. Yes, my Ladybird and my Dragonfly! My creative mind went into overdrive imagining a children's book around these little characters.

The next day I sat down to write, and by the following day my first draft was complete. The words flowed so naturally, it gives me tingles just thinking about it. I could clearly visualise the illustrations I would create to go with the story – bright and whimsical set amongst meadow flowers that I grew up loving. I would use both felting and watercolour to create them. Eagerly that night I read the first draft of *Ladybird and Dragonfly: The Birthday Surprise* to my daughters and husband. Elena could see herself in the character of Ladybird. I saw their little faces engaging with the story and I knew I had created something special. It was the most glorious feeling.

Georgina introduced me to Amy, the fabulous founder of Mamas in Biz. Amy welcomed me into a growing community of inspirational women. Amongst these women was Natalia Hooker, the founder of Alaya Books, editor and author. It was meant to be! My first call with Natalia filled me with nerves. I loved my manuscript, and I was desperate for her to see its potential. Thankfully, she said she adored it and graciously took it on. My book would come to life. Weirdly, this wasn't scary; in fact, it was exciting, even the niggling voice was silent! A warm feeling overtook me.

I realised that the universe had brought me here. Every path, every aspect of my life had led to this wonderful moment of unfurling. I was supposed to go through the struggles as a good girl and break free. I was supposed to meet and marry Andres and create our beautiful family. I was supposed to move to Spain, meet Georgina, Amy, and Natalia, and become part of Mamas in Biz.

It has been tough, but I have finally learnt to believe in my artistic abilities. To take ownership of my creativity and develop my business *Creations by Lois* around it. Who knows what else is to come!

Lois Ireland
@creations_bylois
Etsy: FeltingEarthbyLois

MONICA BUZALI

"Remember, you always get what you want."

I sat on the edge of the bed until I felt comfortable, sinking into the mattress. A cool breeze came in through the vents in my room; the colour of the space embraced me. Several years before, during my adolescence, I had decided that grass green was *MY* colour, and therefore, all the furniture had to be in that tone. My mom agreed, although she was never happy with the decision, but who would want to argue with a determined fifteen-year-old?

So that morning, I sat on my green bed, with a green quilt, looking in front of me at my green bookshelf, and I sighed. I was tired, frustrated, and disappointed.

A few months earlier, I had broken up with my boyfriend, or rather, *HE* had broken up with me. A complicated relationship where I always felt like I loved him more, always insecure about his love for me, and always trying to be someone other than myself. He moved overseas, to New York City, and I was open and excited to join him, but then he met someone else.

When he told me, my body froze, motionless. On the outside, everything seemed intact, like a statue, but on the inside, I was falling apart. My stomach was the first to go, then my heart and brain began to disintegrate and slide away like sand inside an hourglass. The rest of my insides melted, leaving only the exterior of an empty figure.

That's how I stayed for weeks, stuck in my green-furnished room, under my green sheets, breathing in my own carbon dioxide. Suddenly, *MY* green no longer sparkled, it had turned dark and thick, like oil.

The days passed, and I started to blend in with the bed, but little by little, I began to peel myself away, like chewing gum stuck to a wall... with a spatula and a lot of patience. I started going to therapy and breathing – almost at the same time. I stopped crying every day and began to fantasise about the idea of moving out of my parents' house and into an apartment on my own.

Given the circumstances, one day my parents sat down to talk with me. "You wanted to go to another country to study, now you want to move out on your own?" "Do you know what you want? How can we help you?" "Leave Mexico, we'll support you." "You can do it, you've been planning and searching for a long time – maybe it's time to take the leap."

Their voices carried a hint of concern, even though they were doing everything they could to sound confident and sure.

And so began my mission: 'escape the miserableness' and figure out where to go. I wanted somewhere where I'd feel familiar with the culture, and I started looking at Spain. I didn't know the country, I just knew I could speak my language there. I imagined the culture would be similar to Mexico's.

So Barcelona became my final destination. Why? I could say it was 'chance', although I don't really believe in chance, especially not after everything that's happened to me in this city since I arrived, but at the time, that's what it seemed like.

We don't realise how life works in our favour until we're able to look back with perspective. When I was deep in my depression, with no desire or hope for life, I swore I'd never get up again, that my world would stay grey. And I know it sounds cliché and that everyone goes through this, but I'm very much a drama queen, and I couldn't see the end of my pain. I stayed hooked to that feeling for a long time, even when I was supposedly 'fine', I was still unwell. Exhausting!

During that time, I was seeing a therapist, Martin, a chain-smoking angel who accompanied me through my heart-rebuilding process. We worked on many things, and one of the most important was being able to open myself up again to receive a partner in my life. It was my healing process after heartbreak, and also one of the most powerful tools he gave me to begin my new path.

"Don't ask, give thanks. If you ask, you're standing in lack. If you give thanks, you're assuming that what you want already exists and is there for you," he said in his little magical elf voice. He asked me to write a letter listing all the qualities I was looking for in a partner, in a person, and in a relationship, and to write it in the present tense:

I have a partner:

- who I have a lot of fun with;
- who is good, kind, and has a generous heart;
- who I have incredible sex with and we both enjoy, have fun, and expand together;
- with whom I am free to be who I am, and they are free to be who they are.

So I made a very long and very detailed list (now I realise that since I was already thanking the universe, I could've been more specific in certain areas and spared myself some difficulties, but everything is a learning experience), always in gratitude, excited that this person was out there, wandering the world, about to meet me.

That's why I don't think chance had anything to do with me coming to Barcelona – it was more like a series of very fortunate events and a few helpful nudges from certain people.

Anyway, back to the topic – why Barcelona? While researching what I wanted to do, I came across a master's programme in cultural management, one in Barcelona. Barcelona has the sea, and I had always wanted to live near the sea.

I knew about Gaudí and his work in Barcelona; I had a couple of books I loved to look at, gifts from my dad, who was an architect. When I was little and we'd go to the beach, we'd sit in the sand to play. My dad would fill a bucket with sand and water, grab a handful of the mix, and delicately drip it onto our sandcastles, creating incredible sculptures that looked like melted ice cream or chocolate. He would say, "In Barcelona, there was an architect named Antonio Gaudí who built houses with shapes just like these..." Sometimes he'd talk about the colours, the forms, the stories, the materials he used, always sharing a different detail. I became fascinated by this architect who built as if his spaces belonged in fantasy stories.

A reply came from the University of Barcelona, and that's how I decided to move to a city I had never visited. It could've been the ugliest city in the world (with some pretty Gaudí buildings, but everything else total crap), but my decision was made.

Things I have to do: reply to the acceptance email, send the documents (I'm already late with that), and tell my parents what's going to happen. What have I done? Nothing, nothing, nothing. I haven't done anything. I really want to leave, but I'm panicking, frozen. I want to go, but I do nothing, and the days go by.

My parents ask me how everything is going, and I tell them they haven't replied yet. *What the hell is wrong with me? Wasn't this what I wanted?* No, I wanted to go to New York to live with the other guy, but that ship sailed, exploded into pieces, sank on top of me, and its sharp metal wreckage tore through my guts. I wanted to live the teenage fantasy. I wanted to be Carrie Bradshaw in *Sex and the City* and have my New York fling with Mr Big, to go live with a boyfriend in New York as if I were in a movie (back then we weren't as aware of how much romantic comedies mess with our lives).

I kept thinking that was still going to happen, that the guy would reconsider and call me, beg me to come with him, and we'd live a grand love story. So...

Barcelona, unknown city, it's nothing personal, I'm not considering you, because the moment I say yes to you, I shut the door on the other option – and I not ready to let go of that fantasy.

I rested on my laurels, and waited so long that I got a message from the university:

```
Dear Monica,
The application deadline passed last week. We regret to inform you that you'll only be able to apply for next year.
```

DAMN IT!!!

I had missed the deadline to send the documents. That's when I realised the monumental screw-up I was making, waiting for something that was never going to happen. I had to take charge of my life, but I didn't know how.

I sat on the edge of the bed until I felt comfortable, sinking into the mattress. A cool breeze came in through the vents in my room; the colour of the space embraced me... I breathed and let myself cry, full of frustration and disappointment.

"Moni, are you okay? Can I come in?"

My dad stood in the doorway – calm, patient, loving. He came over and sat next to me. The bed sank, and my body leaned into him. He hugged me, and I rested my head on his shoulder.

"What's going on? Tell me what's wrong."

"I'm not ready," I said. "I'm really sad. I can't get out of this place. I don't know how. I missed the deadline, and now I have to wait another year to go to Barcelona. The registration period is over. I think I waited on purpose so I wouldn't have to go. Maybe I want to keep being miserable and not take responsibility for what's happening to me. I don't know how to do it differently."

My dad got up from the bed, sat down in the green chair at the green desk in front of me, looked at me gently but firmly and said: "You're going to write them an email right now and tell them you missed the deadline due to personal reasons. Ask them to please give you a few more days to submit all the documents. If they say no, then we'll see what to do, but do everything you can to make things happen the way you want them to. Remember, you always get what you want."

That last sentence was a monument in my relationship with my dad. Since I was little, he has always told me that. He used to say that when I was about three years old, we were at a theatre in California, and I had to walk across a row of seats. He thought I wouldn't dare and that I'd end up asking for help. The space was really tight, I didn't speak English, the path was long, and I'd have to walk through a lot of people. How would I manage? How would I ask for permission to pass?

He said he didn't see me worried, that I just started walking and as I did, I looked at each person and smiled. And so, they moved to make space for me. "With your smile and just being yourself, you always get what you want," he'd say every time he told the story.

My dad pushed me to do things. He always had. He had wanted to do many things that weren't conventional for his family and environment, but he chose to follow the rules of his community and build a family the 'right' way. And he was happy. But I think that, in many moments, he would've liked to break free and do things differently from 'the plan', but his commitment to tradition and family won out.

Mr Beto Buzali was a second-generation Mexican, descendant of Syrian Jewish migrants who arrived in the early twentieth century and had to build a new life in a completely unknown place. A conservative family with strong, deeply rooted traditions, and attached to customs. The clan was the most important thing, and because of that, everyone had to do what everyone else did.

It wasn't easy for him to encourage me to leave. A single woman of 'marriageable age' (twenty-three years old), by our family's standards, going off to live alone, was unthinkable. But he pushed me, encouraged me to have big dreams – sometimes too big for what he might have preferred, and to do everything I could to make them come true.

Now I know that, deep down, he was breaking a little at the thought of being apart from me. And he was scared that what I was doing might not be right.

A few days later, I received an email from the master's office at the University of Barcelona. In a nutshell, it said: "Send all your documents as soon as possible. Schedule an interview with the master's director. Make the corresponding enrollment payment, and... we'll see you in October."

WHAT!? It's done... It's done... IT'S DONE!

I still had a lot to do, but I had taken the first steps toward my new life. I was on my way to board a plane that would take off in October 2004, headed to Barcelona, with no return ticket.

Years later, chatting with my daughter and son, I jokingly, but seriously, told them that they exist thanks to their grandpa Beto. That spring day, sitting in my green room, my dad gave me one of the most important nudges of my life and encouraged me to take the step that changed my path forever. Because if I hadn't made that decision, I never would have met their father – the person I've shared the past twenty years with, who transformed my understanding of love and relationships, and with whom I built the family and the life I have today.

In many ways, everything we are now traces back to that moment and to the courage my dad inspired in me. And now, as an art therapist, I weave together tarot, meditation, astrology, and spiritual connection to support individuals, couples, and groups of all ages in their personal journey.

Monica Buzali
@monicabuzali_arteterapia
www.monicabuzali-arteterapia.org

MISCHÉ HAMILTON

"Keep your curtains open, because somewhere out there is a sky worth waking up for."

I could hear the weight and power in each step, yet they landed quietly, amplified by the kind of pitch-black night you only get far from light pollution, and tonight, without even a sliver of moonlight, the darkness swallowed everything whole. The stars were spectacular, yes, but I was beginning to regret my choice of sleeping beneath nothing more than a flimsy mosquito net.

During my years working as an overland safari guide, this had always been my favourite way to sleep out in Botswana's Okavango Delta. It gave just enough shelter, but not so much that you missed the sky waking up.

We had reached our camp on the Delta in mokoros, traditional dug-out canoes poled silently through reed-lined channels. Our polers – local Batswana who knew this bush in their bones – would normally keep a fire burning through the night to ward off animals. They carried no weapons; this was wild camping in every sense. Tonight, though, the fire had burned low, they were all fast asleep, and the footsteps circling camp seemed to go unheard.

I lay rigid, my body still wired from earlier that day. While the clients had gone out on a bush walk with the lead poler, one of the younger men had asked if my driver and I wanted to see buffalo across the stream. Of course we did! A short glide in the mokoro, a quick walk through the bush, and we were standing on top of a termite mound, watching the herd across the channel. Minutes later, my driver's sharp whisper cut the air:

"Don't move. There's a lion."

No more than ten metres away, walking straight toward us was a male lion. My entire body froze. We didn't even have a stick. His gaze locked on the buffalo, but then he noticed us. He stopped. Stared. Seconds stretched like hours. And then, with a flick of his tail, he turned and ran into the bush. We wasted no time in hurrying back to camp with adrenaline still humming through me.

Could these be his footsteps now? They circled slowly, purposefully, along the camp's edge. My heart pounded so loud I feared it would give me away. A few torch beams flicked through the tent flaps, proof I wasn't imagining it. Then the footsteps stopped.

Silence. Heavy, suffocating silence. Every nerve in me screamed.

Suddenly a screech tore through the night. A blood-chilling, guttural gurgle that I can still feel in my bones. The polers shot up, throwing branches onto the fire until it roared back, shadows leaping across camp. And then... silence again.

Lying beneath my mosquito net, eyes fixed on the fire, somewhat comforted by the fact that the polers were now awake, I waited. Slowly, the sky shifted. Black turned to purple, then pink, then finally the burning orange of daybreak. With the light came circling shadows above, vultures.

Not far from our campsite, a lion had killed a buffalo.

That was back in 2001, and it still stands out as one of the most unforgettable sunrises of my life.

I always sleep with the curtains open. Not because I'm forgetful, but because I love waking up to light. I want to be woken by that early morning glow, to feel the start of a brand new day before the world has even rubbed its eyes. I feel cheated if I wake up and it's already mid-morning!

My love of early mornings had taken hold long before my adult years. When I was a child, every June school holidays, we would set off on a two-day drive from Cape Town to my Oupa's (grandpa's) game farm on the edge of Kruger National Park. My parents would bundle us four kids into our VW Kombi at 4:30 a.m., the back seats flattened for sleeping – no seatbelts required in those days.

I'd lie there watching the stars through the back window, then see the Karoo slowly revealed in first light. The Karoo is a vast, semi-arid region in South Africa – it is harsh, sparse, and yet achingly beautiful, especially at daybreak. Those dawn drives carved out my love for the sheer magic of sunrise.

Later, in my early twenties, working as an overland safari guide across Southern and East Africa, I got to sleep under a blanket of stars every night, catch sunrises, and spend my days filled with adventure, travel, and a whole lot of fun. It was there that I met my all-time favourite safari client...

On our very first night of that trip, we camped at Fish River Canyon in Namibia, where the sky exploded with more shooting stars than I've ever seen in my life. Maybe the universe was cheekily hinting that this guy would one day become my partner in chasing sunrises, adventures, and eventually becoming a family of four.

A hop, skip, and a few adventures later, we (favourite client and I) moved to London, worked hard for two years, saved up, and then threw it all in the air for a year of full-blown, full-hearted travels. From dawn swims on sun-drenched Vietnamese beaches to dusty bus rides into the unknown, we collected stories that made our souls sing. We spent three unforgettable months in India, swept up in its colour, chaos, kindness, and contradiction – the culture cracked our hearts wide open. We shared our adventures with friends and family in a private Facebook group filled with snapshots and salty-haired smiles, and story entries typed out whenever the Wi-Fi was strong enough and the inspiration too big to hold in.

The final destination of our trip was Mexico, where we immersed ourselves in Spanish classes for two months and then travelled for another month proudly testing out our brand-new language skills. Eventually, we landed in Barcelona, a city that felt like it had been waiting for us the whole time. Our backpacks dusty and bursting with dreams, our smattering of Spanish navigating a world of Catalan. We arrived in 2009, in the midst of the financial crisis, wrestling with endless paperwork and language blunders, but slowly, roots took hold. And happily, Spanish life suited us.

Now, we speak Spanish, are comfortable with Catalan, and our kids, born here in Barcelona, are fluent in three languages and gleefully correct our language mistakes when needed. It's been a gift, but a hard-earned one. As I've learned again and again: the harder the climb, the more beautiful the view.

Photography didn't come into my life in one big burst, but instead arrived more like a slow-burning campfire. After thirteen years working in African tourism, I realised I wanted to start capturing the beauty in the day-to-day. I'd always been drawn to images, to light, to emotion, and once I began, I couldn't stop. That was in 2015, and I've loved it more every day since.

It's never been about the perfectly posed photo for me. I'm drawn to the real, the wild giggles, the windswept hair, the tear that catches the light just right. I photograph life in motion: bold, vibrant, unfiltered, and full of emotion. I've captured surprise engagements, the incredible power of women in birth, cake-covered toddlers, and personal branding photos that feel honest and electric.

I've watched families grow, returning each year to mark time with me through my lens. And the backdrop? Barcelona, sun-soaked and soul-filled, has given me a canvas like no other and as the seasons change, so does my canvas. No two shoots are ever the same, and this is what I love.

And then, when we began travelling as a family, my camera naturally turned towards my own story. During our first backpacking trip with our boys in Sri Lanka, I stood on Pidurangala Rock, my youngest of one and a half years strapped to my back, camera hanging from my neck, breathless from both the hike and awe of the moment. The sunrise exploded with wild pinks and purples, the kind of light that doesn't just appear, but arrives. At first I didn't want to watch it through my camera lens; I wanted to fully take it in (and catch my breath!). But once I had unstrapped my littlest, I couldn't resist capturing the moment, my three loves (hubby and sons) backed by sunrise on top of a rock in Sri Lanka.

We had woken at 4 a.m. for this prize, climbed in the dark with head torches. My heart could explode. I felt so happy! Bathed in the start of morning sunlight, a trickle of sweat from my brow, heart still pounding from the exertion and joy, something clicked. Maybe it was the shutter, or maybe it was just my whole being saying: *this is it.* These are the moments I want to chase.

Becoming a mother had shifted things for me somewhat. Travelling with my boys made me more aware of time, of fleeting moments, and what I wanted to give them. Not things. Not a highlight reel. But a way of seeing. I want them to be rich in experiences, empathy, and wonder. To notice the taste of something new, or the way someone's eyes light up when they speak their truth. To understand that even the smallest act of giving back matters. To not just travel, but to really see and never take it for granted.

That realisation became the spark for my next adventure, Zwela. From photographing my kids' childhoods, capturing the big and small moments, to creating a way for children everywhere to do the same. In 2024, with my talented friend and artist, Kat Cameron, we launched *Zwela Journals - Kids Travel Journals,* which invite children to pause, reflect, and engage their senses; to feel, to wonder, and to grow. They encourage gratitude, empathy, and mindfulness, giving children a space to tell their own stories and capture their truth. Because travel isn't just about the places we go, but the people we become along the way. And most importantly, they remind kids that every day is an adventure, it all depends on how you embrace it.

One of my life's successes so far? The fact that my boys eagerly wake to watch the sunrise (I am very aware we still have the teenage years to come, but I take the win for what it is now, right in this moment). They don't groan when I drag them out of bed to watch the sky catch fire. They get it, and most times they are equally excited for a sunrise swim, as long as I don't forget the snacks! And these moments, that's the best photo I'll ever take, be it mentally or with my camera.

What I've learned from this wild, light-chasing, language-learning, deeply beautiful journey so far, is that you don't need to have it all figured out. You just need to start. Say yes.

Chase the sunrise, laugh when it all goes sideways, take the leap, follow your dreams, and keep your curtains open. Because somewhere out there is a sky worth waking up for.

Mische Hamilton
@by_mish
@zwelajournals
www.bymishphotography.com
www.zwelajournals.com

JOHANNA OVALLES

"Being healthy is simple, easy, and it all begins by going back to basics."

I was born in Maracay, Venezuela, but when I was a young girl, we moved to Florida in the United States. Gainesville, the city of the gators, became our home because my father was doing his postgraduate studies there.

I spent most of my childhood and teenage years in Florida, and to this day, some of the most beautiful memories of my early life belong to that time and place. But my life was always divided between the United States and Venezuela.

My heart belonged to both countries, but at the same time, I never truly felt I belonged to either one. In Venezuela, they called me *'la gringa'* because I spoke English. In the United States, I was simply an immigrant – it was never really 'my country'. I've always believed that we each come into this world with a purpose. And deep down, I've always felt that my purpose is to help others.

That's what led me to study law in Venezuela. I was so in love with the idea of *ius aequum*, the kind of justice that is fair, humane, and truly equal for everyone. But I later realised that what I had studied and what I experienced in practice were two very different things.

In reality, the law is often interpreted based on convenience, not integrity or true justice. I became completely disenchanted with the profession I had once pursued so passionately. And so, I put away my degree and that chapter of my life, as one more memory from a stage that no longer reflected who I truly was in my values and in my essence. Then life gave me, unexpectedly, the most beautiful profession I could have ever imagined: becoming a mother.

And I say unexpectedly, because I wasn't looking for it

I was in one of the darkest periods of my life, completely lost, going through a deep depression after the recent loss of my father, who had meant everything to me. He wasn't just my father, he was my mentor, my safe space, and the one person who truly understood me and knew how to speak to me. He was a deeply cultured man, someone who always had an answer for everything. He taught me to love good music like jazz and bossa nova, and he passed on to me his passion for studying, for learning, for growing. And he also made me laugh. His presence in my life shaped so much of who I am. Losing him broke something deep inside me. But it also opened the door to a new kind of strength I didn't know I had.

And just like that, life, the universe, and what I love to call God, gave me the greatest gift: my daughter. She was a sign that whispered: *keep living... your story is just beginning.* And it truly was.

I was reborn the day she was born, finding a new and deeper meaning to this journey we call life on earth.

Then came another big chapter in my life: emigrating. But this time, it wasn't just moving between my two comfort zones – the United States and Venezuela – it was "crossing the ocean," as we say in my country.

I moved to Spain, which has now become my home.

Barcelona stole my heart, and for the first time in my life, I felt truly at home. Now, I can honestly say I'm a citizen of the world, carrying a little piece of each culture within me.

The process of migration was far from easy. I arrived without family – everyone I loved was still in the Americas. I had to figure everything out on my own. My husband is a pilot, often away flying for days at a time. I found myself in a new country with a small child, learning in real time what it truly means to be a mother, because no one ever teaches you that part.

I wasn't just navigating motherhood in a foreign land, without a support network, and with a partner often absent... I was also beginning a deep and silent battle with my health.

For as long as I can remember, I spent years going from gynaecologists to gastroenterologists. I was hospitalised countless times due to unexplained pain – symptoms that never came with a clear diagnosis. It was always "just stress," or "you probably have a low pain threshold." Until finally, my pain had a name: Endometriosis.

A complicated name I had never heard before, but one that validated what I had been feeling for years. And no, it wasn't that my pain threshold was too low. With that diagnosis, my story of resilience began... and my journey back to myself.

It was an incredibly difficult process. Endometriosis is not just something that shows up during your period. It's a condition that affects your body, and your life, every single day. Not just physically, but emotionally too. The pain is constant. I had a stabbing sensations in my ovaries. It felt like something was pulling down from inside me, like I was being torn apart.

A deep, crushing pressure at times extended all the way from my pelvis down my leg. On those days, even the simplest movements felt like climbing a mountain. I had constant fatigue – a heavy, draining exhaustion that made even opening my eyes feel like a battle. Every morning, I would pray for strength – the strength of an eagle, like the Bible says – to get through the day and care for my daughter.

My emotions were on a rollercoaster. I felt like a prisoner inside my own body. The pain had taken over my life.

The medications prescribed to me felt almost worse than the condition itself. They came with intense side effects. The nausea was constant. My stomach always felt sick and bloated, and I was vomiting at least twice a day. The nausea would trigger episodes of tachycardia and near-fainting, due to the activation of my vagus nerve – something I've struggled with for years. When it flares up due to stomach issues, my blood pressure drops so drastically that I often lose consciousness.

And in the middle of those episodes, my mind repeated the same thought over and over: *You have to be okay. Your daughter only has you.* It was terrifying.

Every time it happened, I would lock myself in the bathroom, turn the water on so she wouldn't hear, and grab alcohol and ice to try to bring myself back as fast as I could. The migraines and the dizzy spells were torture. I felt anxious and depressed. I didn't recognise myself anymore. And worst of all? The endometriosis pain didn't go away, not even slightly.

One of the other medications I was prescribed made me feel completely sedated. I couldn't stay awake and I felt drugged all the time.

That was the final straw. That's when I knew I had to take back control of my healing. I knew I had to find another way.

Those were dark days. But even then, there was one light: my daughter. Just hearing her name reminded me that I needed to keep going. That I had to be okay. I was determined to give her a happy childhood – one where she wouldn't have to see how broken her mother truly felt. And I did.

I believe that whenever we receive a diagnosis, any diagnosis, we are faced with two paths. To live it from a place of LOVE, by accepting what we are going through and walking the journey with awareness. Or to live it from a place of FEAR, by denying what we feel and letting our worst-case thoughts take control. When you choose to see in the light, even in the most difficult moments, you are redirecting your energy towards true healing.

My story is one of love. The love I have for my daughter gave me the strength to look for alternatives. I knew I couldn't keep going like this. I needed to support my body in a way that was kinder, safer... more aligned with who I am.

I made a choice: to educate myself about my condition, to understand it, and to find a way to support my body with more kindness, without suffering the devastating side effects of conventional treatments.

I dove deep into studying nutrition, the microbiome, and everything I could find that would help me heal. I studied relentlessly, as if I were trying to piece together a giant puzzle. That curious, investigative side of me, I inherited it from my father, my greatest role model.

And I reached a powerful conclusion: being healthy is so simple that perhaps that's exactly why many doctors and the pharmaceutical industry don't want us to know it.

It's simple, it's affordable, and it all begins by going back to the basics:

Hugs – to release hormones that regulate cortisol.

Sunlight.

Restorative sleep.

Emotional awareness.

Movement – so that energy can also move.

Eating mindfully and naturally – avoiding ultra-processed foods.

Life is much simpler than we think. And so is our path to wellness. We just need to return to the essentials.

I began integrating all these habits into my daily life. But due to my hormonal imbalances, I developed such severe insomnia that I barely slept three hours a night. With a four-year-old to care for, it was an incredibly challenging stage.

Just before the pandemic, I told a close friend what I was going through, and she said she would send me an essential oil as a gift to support me. I told her not to bother, that I had always loved essential oils, but I saw them mostly as something that smelled nice and helped you relax a little. I even joked that I lived in Spain, not in some desert where nothing was available, and that I had already tried several oils without any results.

I am deeply grateful that my friend didn't listen to me and sent it anyway, because it changed my life. Until then, I didn't truly understand their real power.

The parcel arrived just two days before the lockdown began, and what a blessing it was. My body was completely exhausted. I needed that lockdown – if it hadn't happened, I would have been hospitalised, with no one to care for my daughter. My husband was stuck in the United States for work and couldn't return to Spain. We went eight months without seeing each other.

When I finally had that essential oil in my hands, I followed the instructions exactly: 'Put it on the soles of your feet, on your wrists, and inhale.'

That night, I slept. For the first time in a very long time, I slept through the night. I couldn't believe it.

And then it happened again. I slept.

That's when I saw, with absolute clarity, what had been missing in my healing journey – the missing piece of my healing puzzle.

It allowed me to strengthen and truly affirm the mantra that carried me through that entire process. The one I still repeat to myself today, the one that brings me back to my place of balance:

Everything is fine, and it's going to be fine. I am safe.

I began researching everything related to essential oils and how they could help the symptoms of my endometriosis. I immersed myself in this new, natural world.

Knowledge gives us power. We become our own best doctors when we learn to truly listen to our bodies. And today, thanks to my own story, I feel empowered. This entire process, with every lesson and every fall, led me back to myself. And today, sharing it and supporting other women is my way of giving back to the universe for all the gifts it has given me... for showing me the way, for reminding me who I am, and for teaching me that there is strength in vulnerability.

I am also giving my daughter an example: teaching her to take command of her own health, to connect with herself, to understand the importance of emotions as part of her essential wellbeing, and to trust that the gifts of nature, like essential oils, can be companions and blessings in every area of life.

Today, I have an international business that allows me to impact lives. I am a woman who dedicates her life to helping other women find their own wellbeing, especially those facing hormonal imbalances, stress, and anxiety. In doing so, I feel I am fulfilling my life's purpose.

I hope my story inspires you and reminds you that, no matter how many turns or lows you face in life, you must never lose faith in yourself. Go back to you.

Johanna Ovalles
@theessencespot
www.theessencespot.com

LAURA MORENO

"Never stop learning – there are no limits, only in your mind."

A little girl in her grandmother's house. Opening drawers and cupboards...

She knew where everything was in that house, every single item. Still, she went on, opening and reopening every drawer again. Waiting to find the treasure, a magic stone, something she hadn't seen before. Pulling things out, putting them back carefully, letting each object spark her imagination: *What could I use this for?*

That curious, imaginative mind is still with me now, over forty years later. It has taken me on adventures I never could have planned.

My childhood was turbulent. Since I was two years old, my mother had to be in a psychiatric hospital.

But my story is also her story, and the story of women in Spain in 1975. That was the year my mother had my older brother. The Franco dictatorship was still in power, and women couldn't work, open a bank account, or even drive a car without written permission from their husband or father.

My mother was fiercely independent and working at the time, but the weight of culture and law pulled her back into a role she didn't choose. She was told: *"A good woman stays home with the children."* That broke her. Depression took hold, and over the years, it deepened into manic-depression and bipolar disorder.

I was born in 1977, into a world where my mother was already fighting that battle. So I grew up with my grandmother and aunts near Madrid, in a working-class neighbourhood filled with families who had migrated from all corners of Spain. It taught me resilience, independence, and resourcefulness.

And that same curiosity that pushed me to open drawers, led me to discover boxes of old black-and-white photographs my father kept at home. Family portraits, racing cars, sports. I studied them over and over, fascinated. That was my first spark.

Inspired by those old photographs, I chose to study photography in high school, and later took a big leap: I went to London to study photojournalism. I planned to stay for a year and a half. I stayed for seventeen years.

London was a treasure chest of culture, hidden places, and endless opportunities. I would take a bus or ride my bike and get lost on purpose, just as I did as a little girl searching drawers. My treasure hunt became the hidden streets and magical corners of the city. Before GPS, before Google Maps, it was me, an A-Z map book, and memory. That's how I got to know London, every bus route, every hidden path.

My curiosity stretched even further – to Peru, Colombia, India, Paris, Amsterdam, Berlin, Laos, Thailand, the Himalayas, Portugal... my camera and my mind chasing new stories and new worlds.

But the two greatest adventures of my life weren't on a map. They were entrepreneurship and motherhood.

I never fit into the mould of the typical nine-to-five office job. I tried, I really did. But I was *'un culo inquieto'*, as we say in Spanish, restless, always moving, searching, determined to carve my own path.

I started working at fourteen. My first job? Attaching hard plastic handles to plastic shopping bags. Paid by the piece, and I was fast, a teenager already learning productivity. From there, countless side jobs and trying everything out.

In London, I found a career I loved in web design, IT management, and teaching. It was exciting, creative, and independent.

Until motherhood shook everything.

After my first baby, a beautiful girl, I suddenly saw myself on my mother's path. Postpartum depression hit me hard. London's winter wrapped around me. I felt trapped.

For the first time since I was fourteen, I was financially dependent. And I had a tiny creature completely dependent on me. My world collapsed. My nervous system crumbled.

But I made a decision: *No. This is not my path.* I would not repeat my mother's story. I could choose. I would find a way.

That became the start of a long journey, of searching for a new way, a new why, a new what.

While I was caring for my daughter, I gradually fought my way back with awareness and intention. Depression was real, but so was my determination. I studied again, worked bit by bit, and slowly returned to my passions of teaching and technology.

I always liked to keep things organised, but it wasn't until I started looking into new career paths in Spain that I realised how natural this was for me. Systems, tools, puzzles, I loved figuring out what worked, what didn't, and how to make it fit together.

Then I gave birth to twins, a boy and a girl. Three children under the age of three. My world shifted again.

With them came another big change: we moved back to Spain, settling in Barcelona. Suddenly, I wasn't only navigating motherhood, but also the challenge of creating a new life in a new place.

It was in Barcelona, while trying to settle down and still searching for a new career path, that I truly reconnected with my natural strengths. I realised that what had always been survival tools for me – organisation, systems, technology – was actually a gift I could share.

Then, another turning point came. Vertigo struck. Three days in bed, unable to move, my children were still so little. The frustration of not being able to do anything was overwhelming, especially with so little support around me. I felt invisible. That collapse forced me to see the truth: *If I didn't take care of myself, no one else would.*

It was powerful. From then on, self-care became non-negotiable. And my love for productivity, organisation, and digital tools deepened. These helped me – not only to work less, but to do everything better.

That was when I knew: this is what I'm meant to do. Help women build systems that support them, not crush them, and help them find balance, freedom, and possibility.

Today, my passion is helping women in business:

- To create systems, use digital tools, and embrace AI.
- To work smarter, not harder.
- To build balance without giving up what matters most.

Because we don't have to choose between motherhood and career, or between entrepreneurship and family. We can create our own way.

My mother couldn't choose. But I can. And so can you.

There is no single model of motherhood – full-time, part-time, business-owner, career-woman – only what fits you, your needs, and your desires.

Be adventurous. Have courage. Create the life you want. There are no limits, only in your mind.

Laura Moreno
@laura_moreno
www.laumore.com

LENA MENDEZ

"Even the flap of a butterfly's wings can trigger a tsunami."

Some people seem to be born with a plan for life. Even as teenagers, they know what they want to become, how many kids they'll have, if they'll live in a house with a white-picket fence, and where they'll spend their summer holidays when they are thirty-seven and a half.

That's not me.

Even today, if someone asked, "Where do you see yourself in five years?" I'd kind of freeze. Not for lack of imagination. But because there are so many possibilities. I might have a rough plan for next week, and tomorrow is on the calendar. But five years? Not a clue.

In Berlin as a child and teenager, my ideas of a future job jumped from doctor (hence choosing Latin as a third language - absolutely useless now), to singer, kindergarten teacher, vet... or even better, everything at the same time.

After tenth grade, I switched schools to study psychology for my final exams. One of my first pitiful attempts to understand us human beings and perhaps also to heal my mom, who suffered from anxiety and heavy depression. Twenty-five years later, she still struggles with it, and I never became a psychologist.

It took me three years after high school to finally decide what to study. I studied business administration with a focus on marketing. Why? Honestly, because I didn't know what else to do. I couldn't decide, I couldn't commit to anything. And people said, "With business, you can do almost anything." That sounded perfect for someone like me, being undecided and dancing in my mind from one idea to another.

I finished my studies pretty well, but again: what now? The old combo of self-doubt and an aversion to locking in a decision didn't help.

I signed up with a temp agency (not the usual next step for a new graduate) and landed a six-month project-based job at Daimler Financial Services in Berlin.

From the outside, it looked pretty good. Fresh out of university, working there in a big Berlin skyscraper, part of a global rebranding project, sitting in meetings on big tables with experienced and self-confident people. But inside, I never felt like I belonged there and was always hoping that no one would ask me a question I didn't know the answer to. And I knew quickly this wasn't my path.

I remember sitting in that office, looking down at the streets of Berlin where life was happening, while I was sitting dressed in business clothes, trying to look the part. Before the project ended, they offered me a permanent job. But just thinking about a Monday-to-Friday, suit-wearing, nine-to-five career made me feel trapped. That wasn't me. So I said no.

And, like so often in life, another door opened almost instantly. A contact from the marketing world introduced me to the owner of a small agency. She needed support and was open to working together. I didn't want to be anyone's employee anymore, tied to fixed hours or rules, so I registered my own business and had my first client.

At the same time, something returned to my life: movement.

During my studies, I'd discovered Nia, a barefoot fusion of dance, martial arts, and mindfulness. There were no classes in Berlin, so I'd even written my final business administration thesis on this. I had set myself the task of developing a marketing strategy for Nia to increase awareness within Germany. Eventually, curiosity pushed me to do the teacher training. I did it for myself and to understand this movement concept even better for my thesis - not to actually teach it. But life had its own plans.

Soon, I was teaching Nia, while continuing to support my client at the agency. For the first time, I didn't move just to reach and keep appearance-related goals. Nia awakened my body awareness and slowly opened a new world. My interest for movement, exercise, and all health-related things grew.

Almost without noticing, I started building knowledge – one teacher training, one master class, one workshop at a time. And suddenly, I was no longer wandering in all directions, but following a path that felt right under my feet, literally.

It wasn't just about the doors, it was about the people holding them open. Behind my first freelance project was the agency owner Mandy Davids, now one of my closest friends. Behind my Nia journey, Ann Christiansen, a strong woman who inspired me deeply and was my first role model related to a healthy lifestyle.

Behind the next bigger step was the partner of my best friend, the owner of a well-known health and fitness institute. I spent weekends training at his institute while still working for the agency and teaching classes. Over time, I also helped with marketing behind the scenes and later became a lecturer there, teaching other trainers about business and self-employment.

Then came one of the biggest shifts of all. I became a mum. Eight years before, I had met my partner in the hotel where we had both worked, and at that time I was pretty sure I would never have kids. Suddenly, the desire to start a family came so strongly that I could hardly think about anything else.

Like many women, I thought I'd just keep doing everything as before. And to be honest, I did. My daughter was an easy, peaceful baby, and I started working from home again for the agency just weeks after giving birth. I resumed teaching Nia classes two to three times a week when my baby girl was not even six weeks old. It's not something I recommend, and nothing to be proud of, but back then, I didn't know how to let go. I felt responsible for keeping everything running, to say yes to everything, and to prove to myself that I could do it.

A few more years passed. I continued to develop, both personally and professionally. In the meantime, our small family had grown to three children. I kept juggling roles with work experience and learning, still not sure where it was all going to take me. I decided to share it with someone else. I booked a session with a business coach a friend had recommended. I hoped she'd find something special or could tell me where I should put my focus.

So I answered her questions about my background, shared my doubts, and told her about my struggles with choosing just one path. She asked why I felt I had to choose. That was easy to answer: I'd learned that. In one of my training courses, they explained that offering too many different things would make me look unfocused and have no credibility.

The coach gave me a new perspective. Yes, a lot of specialists in different fields exist and are important, like a heart surgeon. But the world also needs generalists, like a family doctor. People who see connections, ask the right questions, and look beyond narrow lanes – and that's what she saw in me.

She said that my wide-angle curiosity and layered experiences were not my weakness, they were my gift. Even my business studies, which had long felt irrelevant, might one day show up in unexpected ways. She was right.

I stopped trying to trim myself down to fit in a box or meet other people's expectations. I began to see how everything I had learned and experienced serve a purpose. Soon after, I had the chance to bring many of these skills together.

On the brink of 2019, the usual New Year's resolutions started popping up. Less sugar, more vegetables, no sweets, more reading, lose five kilos. I held myself back from my usual eye rolling. I wondered: why do we always go so big, so drastic, when we try to change? What if we focused instead on small steps? Just as the flap of a butterfly's wings can trigger a tsunami, these small things often lead to bigger ones.

And so, little by little, after bedtime, laundry, and clearing up for the day, the idea for my *Ambition Cards* was born. A deck of fifty-two cards, each with one small, doable weekly challenge from areas I'd worked in and lived for years: movement, nutrition, mindset, and sustainability.

An online shop followed. More products were planned. I founded a new business: *Ambitions Lifestyle*, with me as managing director. I accompanied the challenges on Instagram and some on my new podcast *As Heart As Possible*. And without realising it, I created something that would support me just as much as it would support others. It was so exciting! I started to build something meaningful, something I was really proud of.

Then life, quite literally, was put on ice. A worldwide pandemic. A new country and baby number four.

We followed through on a long-held plan to move from Berlin to Barcelona. We had always felt the pull to live somewhere else for a while. Not to escape Berlin, but to experience a different rhythm, culture, and lifestyle. We loved cities such as London, Paris, and Valencia, but with Barcelona, something clicked. Like with people, it was chemistry.

It was July 2020 when we moved our home base to this beautiful city that we had fallen in love with years before. I gave birth six weeks before we left, alone in the hospital due to pandemic restrictions. The world was frozen and uncertain, but somehow, I was in motion, like always.

We learned to navigate Barcelona slowly through lockdowns. But there were days I wondered if the creative, ambitious, and vibrant version of me had stayed behind in Berlin. Deep down, I knew she was still in there.

A few times I tried restarting. I taught a few Nia classes in English – it was a huge milestone for me to teach in another language. I started promoting my *Ambition Cards*. I hosted a retreat for my Berlin Nia students here in Barcelona. But life kept pulling me back again and again. With four kids and away from family and friends, it was a tough and challenging time.

We were rebuilding step by step, connection by connection. We found a baseball club for the kids. We met families who became friends. We stumbled into kickboxing classes, the children started skateboarding sessions. We found *LearnLife*, a school with exceptional teachers, or learning guides as we call them there, and open-minded families – an education community that really felt like a second home. Suddenly, we weren't just visitors anymore. We belonged.

But there was still one piece missing! Me. My voice. My business activities.

That's when I found, or more precisely, my *Ambition Cards* and I were found by Amy Piumarta from Mamas in Biz. Amy didn't just see the product; she saw me. Not as the mother of... or the wife of... but as a woman with a lot of potential. She convinced me to teach again. To host workshops. To show myself. And through this community, I met another wonderful woman. Esther Wanjiku, officially a Social Media Strategist, and in real life an unbelievably uplifting, motivating human being. Together with Amy, Esther has pushed me to show up online without hiding behind my cards or being invisible behind the microphone of a podcast.

Despite the fear, the German accent, and the inner critic, I began to share what I have to give, what matters to me, all that I've learned, and all I want to pass on. Because of them and other amazing women in Mamas in Biz, I flourished.

Now, I bring everything together in one-to-one coaching sessions, online programmes, and through classes for women at all stages of life in a phenomenal female studio called BodyWorxHub. I have finally found and live by the perfect mix of movement, nutrition, mindset, sustainability, motherhood, and business.

I am no longer in search of permission or identity. I am supporting other women to feel physically and mentally strong, and to be prepared for whatever life throws their way in good and challenging times.

Lena Mendez
@ambitions.today
www.lenamendez.com

ESTHER FERNANDEZ

"Being a caregiver: absorbing your loved one's suffering while carrying your own."

We moved to Barcelona in 2021, just after the pandemic. Our son, twenty at the time, was studying there, and our daughter, who was fifteen, had just been selected by the Barça basketball team. It felt like a sign, an opportunity for a new beginning.

Previously, we were living in Montpellier, France, where we owned hotels and could manage things remotely. But truthfully, Montpellier never felt like the city where I wanted my kids to grow up. We had been living in the countryside, and this move to the heart of Barcelona marked a complete shift in lifestyle, from quiet rural life to vibrant city life. We embraced it fully. We were simply happy discovering a new rhythm, new routines, and finally enjoying life in a different way.

After receiving the second COVID vaccine, my husband, Franck, noticed two lumps appear. He had been seeing various doctors, but no one could give a clear diagnosis until one day, during a visit to a specialist, everything changed. That day when everything shifts, when deep down inside you know that something is wrong, yet you bury it as far as you can, hoping that denial will somehow change the outcome.

That day, the drive back to our hospital in France felt endless. Franck was behind the wheel, just like every other appointment listening to Eva Cassidy, but today felt different. We didn't talk about it, didn't even look at each other. But we both knew: today's PET scan was about searching for metastases.

Each door slamming, each footstep echoing in the hall made us both jump. Then he went in, and I was left waiting endlessly, unable to complain, as though my own feelings had no right to exist. Stress. Fear. Uncertainty.

Three agonising hours. I leaned on my friends, chatting with them on my phone. Their support was the only thing helping me survive those unknown hours.

And then he came out exhausted, completely worn out. I wrapped him in my arms. Another wait began, this time two hours, and then the doctor would tell us what he had seen.

It felt like a movie. We were called in, ushered into a cold, impersonal room. A chair, a desk, an invisible barrier between us and the doctor.

Then came the unthinkable words: tumor, malignant, chemotherapy, and radiotherapy.

Words you never think you'll hear. Words that only happen to other people. But then one tiny beam of light: no metastases. It was localised.

We were immediately thrust into the whirlwind of hospitalisation, biopsy appointments, anaesthetist visits... a waking nightmare.

The drive home, three hours of near silence, tears, empty minds, blank stares. Franck managed to express his fear, his confusion.

We informed our children. They waited for us at our favourite little restaurant in Barcelona. But that dinner felt surreal, full of embraces, tears, heavy looks, encouragement, and promises to fight. Fight, but fight what, and how? We didn't know yet. We only knew that a tsunami, both medical and emotional, was about to crash into our lives.

Now we had to wait again for the biopsy results. The tumour that had invaded our lives, his life. No one had invited it; it had made itself at home in his throat, as if it belonged there. But it would have to be evicted both medically and mentally.

A few days later, the call came. The only good news in this nightmare: it was HPV, localised in the throat. We finally knew what it was and how it had arrived. We knew of HPV, we had made the decision to vaccinate our daughter just a year ago, but the COVID pandemic had delayed it. Now I knew without a doubt that the vaccination must not wait.

Next, we had to meet with the oncologist to establish the treatment plan. I made an appointment with the best oncologist in Montpellier.

The days passed but no two were the same. Mornings became the hardest part of the day. Seeing him sad, angry... his eyes said everything.

I had no right to complain. I had to be his rock, his comfort, the one to lift his spirits even when I was heartbroken myself. Life isn't fair. He is kind, always putting others first, and generous. Why him?

The helplessness was unbearable. Sometimes I felt guilty simply for being healthy.

There were long moments of silence when I could feel his despair, his confusion, and all I could do was sit beside him, in silence. I love him so much. He's the love of my life, and there was nothing I could do to take away his pain.

Finally, the oncology appointment came. A day we had both been waiting for to finally have a plan, a timeline, something concrete.

We thought we were prepared. We were not. Nowhere near prepared.

We listened carefully and then came another blow. The doctor explained the process, the side effects, the duration of the treatment... and again, we weren't ready.

Weeks passed – five weeks of treatment.

I had hoped to find time to write each evening - a way to escape the waking nightmare, but I never found the time or the strength. Our days became a steady rhythm of doctor visits, chemotherapy, and radiotherapy sessions. Mornings were tough; preparing fresh fruit that would hopefully taste good enough for him despite the side effects. My only outings were to the pharmacy, supermarket, and doctors.

The drive between Barcelona and Montpellier became harder – pain, discomfort, anxiety. And I was the only person he could vent to. That's the hardest part of being a caregiver: absorbing your loved one's suffering while carrying your own.

I allowed myself two moments of freedom during that time: lunch with a friend and a Pilates class. Even then, I felt guilty for taking time for myself while my love was suffering.

The solitude was crushing.

Friends helped – a grocery run, a quick visit, a kind word. It meant everything. Then there was the family, supportive from afar, taking care of the children, for which I will be eternally grateful. Everyone has their own way of showing compassion and offering help. Some people are very present, while others are absent. We all react differently when faced with challenges. Learning to accept this helped me suffer less and truly appreciate every gesture, big or small.

Days passed. The pain worsened, and new side effects appeared. Sleepless nights, anxiety, fear. For Franck, the horror of living through it. For me, the helplessness of watching and not knowing how to ease his pain.

Sometimes I talked to friends, cautiously, not wanting to burden them with too much sadness.

And then came *the day of too much.* The day when you do everything you can to make things better but it's not enough. The anger comes out – directed at you, the only person there to catch it.

As his wife, his caregiver, I took the blows. And they hurt.

That day, after a rough morning, my husband didn't want to go to radiotherapy. He was upset with my driving, my way of handling things, and I reached my breaking point. I walked to the sea, tears streaming down my face, screaming silently for help.

And then – a hand on my shoulder. It was my friend Jelena, passing by at that very moment. A sign from God, answering my desperate cry.

I cried, ran, walked, and released it all.

I know his anger wasn't truly at me. It's at the illness. But it's so hard.

Everything felt unjust – the illness, the side effects, the loneliness, and the cruelty.

Meanwhile, texts came from the children about school and activities. They didn't know much detail of what we're going through because we chose to shield them.

Messages came from others: *If you need anything, I'm here...* But only my true friends really understood, they were *there* with tissues, comfort food, just the right words.

I'm still standing today, because of them.

When Franck was healing and we were back in Barcelona, when everything in my life felt like it was falling apart, I found myself endlessly scrolling on my phone, trying to find something to hold on to. That's when I stumbled across Mamas in Biz. I started following their posts quietly until one day, I saw an invitation to an event in a library. I had never done anything like that before, but something inside told me I needed to go to break through the loneliness.

So I did.

I walked into that room full of women I didn't know. When it was my turn to introduce myself, a few words came out, but mostly, it was tears. I was embarrassed, but also deeply moved. These women, each of them, had their own stories, their own struggles, and they embraced me in a way I didn't expect. It was a turning point for me. The beginning of reclaiming my place in the world, not just as a caregiver or a wife in crisis, but as a woman who still had something to offer and something to rebuild.

That was a turning point for me. I needed that push, I needed to belong somewhere, and most of all, I needed to exist for myself. Not just as a wife, a mother, or a caregiver, but as a woman with her own identity.

Around that time, a friend invited me to a business presentation. I decided to go. After everything we'd been through, I knew I had to get out of the hotel business. I needed something of my own, something that made sense for *me*. I will always be thankful to her, because that day, I made a decision: to take care of myself and build something new.

Franck's illness, combined with the pandemic, had made things incredibly difficult for our hotels. Eventually, my husband made the painful decision to let them go. It was a hard moment for him, letting go of what he had built, and I knew I had to step in and support our family financially.

My new business, *Nu Skin*, brought me everything I was missing. It gave me purpose. It helped me feel more confident again. Step by step, I managed to build my own team, to grow and to rise.

Nu Skin didn't just give me products – it gave me a business I could build on my own terms. It's allowed me to start fresh, create new connections, and help other women feel good in their skin while building their own path too.

If I look back at the Esther who walked into that library that day, and compare her to the woman I am today, I can say that I'm proud of the journey she's made. It hasn't been easy, far from it. But every step, every tear, every moment of doubt was worth it. Because today, I stand stronger, freer, and more aligned with who I truly am.

Esther Fernandez Galvan
@estherfdezgalvan

STEPHANIE VAN STEIJN

"Not giving up is the way to make dreams happen."

I am a jack of all trades, master of none. And honestly, I'm proud of it. I've worn many hats, and I've learned something from every one of them. Hostess. Technical service. Petting zoo keeper. Office manager.

Personal assistant. Now? I'm learning the ropes of trading – deep diving into charts, strategies, and mindset. People are often surprised. That a smiling hostess knows how to hold her ground and gets shit done. That a woman can split logs, speak up, and handle more than she 'looks like she can'.

But here's the thing: I don't do it to prove a point. I do it because I'm curious, capable, and not afraid to start something new. I'm not trying to master one thing. I'm just here to keep growing – and trading happens to be my current path.

I always said I wanted to live abroad. Since I was sixteen, I'd talk about moving to Italy or Spain – and somehow, Spain just felt right. At the time, I was living in North Holland with my parents and had never even been on a plane. So it's always surprised me how strong that feeling was, despite having no experience to base it on.

Twelve years later, I finally made it happen. And even though the work I was supposed to move for was cancelled, and at the same time I found out my grandmother had passed away... even after that setback and sad moment, I knew I still had to go. The company that cancelled my original job offered me work in Amsterdam, hoping to keep me within the company. But I knew if I didn't leave then, I never would.

I arrived in Barcelona on a Monday, and managed to get hired that same day by a different company. Although I'd always had jobs I enjoyed in the Netherlands – receptionist, office assistant, hostess – my first actual job in Barcelona ended up being in customer service. Not ideal, but I've always done what I needed to do to move forward.

That first walk along the beach in Barcelona felt surreal. The buildings, the energy, the palm trees – everything amazed me. I didn't recognise the feeling at first, but then it hit me: this feels like HOME. It was something I had never felt before. Barcelona felt like the place I was meant to be.

I had a hotel booked until Thursday with my mum, who came with me for the first couple of days. I really hoped I'd have an apartment by Friday... Friday morning, I still had no rental contract signed for an apartment. Where would I sleep? I couldn't afford to stay in a hotel any longer. But then – just in time – I got a message. A room in a shared apartment was available. I could move in that day. See? Everything works out, like always.

During my second year in Barcelona, I even did something I'd always wanted to do: I organised a ten-day litter cleanup around my neighbourhood. I'd been too shy to do something like that in the past, but here, in Barcelona, it felt natural – and incredibly fulfilling. People would stop to thank me, and I felt proud. I was doing something good. I belonged. I even raised some money for an ocean cleanup. It's ironic as I had sworn off picking up litter after I worked at a campsite and had to clean people's trash every day. But it frustrated me over the years to see that nobody cleans up litter in some places, so I decided to be the one to do it.

Eventually, I had to return to the Netherlands. I had a plan - to save money so I could come back and buy my own place in Spain. When the airport taxi arrived and I had to leave my tiny apartment in Barcelona, I cried. I'd never been that sad to leave a place. I cried for two weeks straight. Because I wasn't just leaving a city, I was leaving home.

Back in the Netherlands, life moved fast. I got a job, got pregnant, gave birth, and planned my return to Spain before my maternity leave ended. I sold my house in the Netherlands and went back to Spain, the place where my heart lived. Initially, Valencia was the plan, but that just turned into a five-week holiday. Barcelona felt more like the right place to live. But it was in Valencia where I continued to do cleanups, almost on a daily basis. I would walk with my baby strapped to my chest and clean along the shoreline. Its the last place litter is before it ends up in the ocean where it's harder to find – I think that's why cleaning beaches is so rewarding. Since then, I made myself a promise to always leave the beach cleaner than I found it.

Not long after returning, my life shifted again. I became a single mom. No family nearby, no close friends, but I had my everything: my son.

Thanks to some early choices, my parents, and managing money well, I was able to buy a home here without a mortgage. That financial freedom has shaped everything. From the outside, it may look like just luck. But behind it was discipline, timing, and sacrifice. I didn't party much, I planned carefully, and I made it work. It allowed me to start again – on my terms. But I am also a big believer in following instinct, which was a big part of this process as well.

Somewhere in the midst of it all, I launched a passion project I'd been dreaming about for years: *The Green Spirit*. It's an Instagram page and website focused on sustainable living. It's not a business (yet), but it's something that matters deeply to me. I have notebooks full of content ideas and so many things that I need to put into action, and I know that I'm not giving up on this.

It's so silly to think we have to buy everything from the supermarket in plastic. I go to the fruit store all the time with my reusable bags, jars, and fruit bags, walking out with only the broccoli wrapped in plastic. I'm not going to tell you 'vegan is the way', because I believe it's not what we eat but how it is produced and where.

It would be amazing if we all try to buy mainly local, organic, natural, and seasonal products; it would do the world of good. When I daydream about this project, I dream about the many people I could inspire, people sharing their story of what they have changed to live more sustainably, maybe having an online shop, and also sharing my knowledge in person. How amazing would it be if my story could ripple outward, inspiring others the way seeds spread across a meadow. The results would be cleaner neighbourhoods, more space for nature, and more support for local businesses.

People and companies who inspire me are definitely 'The Ocean Cleanup', 'Elho', and Dirk Groot better known as 'the Zwerfinator' in the

Netherlands. It's not just the big companies that are making a change, but also the individual people who play an important part in this.

People need to know that making small changes doesn't have to be expensive or hard. Small shifts, like growing herbs in your own garden, which is cheaper (and better) than buying plastic-wrapped supermarket ones. Imagine if eight billion people made just a ten percent change for the planet. The impact would be massive.

Another important question I thought of a couple of years ago was, *Would I want this planet for a child?* The answer was no, for a while. I seriously doubted if I wanted to have children, because what world is out there for them right now? Processed food is more and more accepted, plastic is everywhere (even in unborn embryos and human brains), welfare diseases, and the culture of fast fashion. And there is no clear sign that things will change for the better.

However, now that I do have a son, this motivates me to make the world a better place, to not give up on my passion project, and to set the right example. This is why my target audience is young adults and families. I truly believe we have the best shot of turning things around by giving the right example to and educating the youth.

But I am also studying to become a trader. People would ask why I don't just schedule my *The Green Spirit* content or my study time better. I didn't know the answer, but in 2024, I was diagnosed with ADHD, and suddenly, everything made sense. The chaos in my head, the hyperfocus followed by brain fog, the creative bursts. It's all part of how I'm wired. My brain isn't broken, it's just wired differently. I've learned to work with it, not against it. I don't like labels, but by understanding there is a different manual than society gave me, life just gets a bit easier.

Work-wise, it hasn't been easy. I live outside my home country, raise my son alone, and don't speak Catalan. My Spanish is still in progress. Finding work that suits my lifestyle and accepts English or Dutch has been difficult. But I stay open. I take what I can, whether it's a one-time job or a short-term project. I trust that with the right mindset, I'll keep moving forward.

Being a working mom without my family living close by to help out and my friends in the Netherlands has been tough. But most days, I don't let it get me down. I stay flexible. I remind myself: yes, I'm tired, yes, I haven't slept in months, but I also matter. Besides that, the thought of me being sick with no one else to take care of my son really motivates me to do some self-care.

I noticed that moms often excuse themselves or feel like they have to explain themselves if they have an afternoon off or day for themselves, but this is so important! Whether you are alone, have a partner, or have the whole family to help you out... don't forget to look after yourself!

Taking care of myself is essential. I might not have a lot to spend, but I manage my money well. That means when my back hurts, I book a massage. When my mind is overloaded, I find a yoga workshop. When I'm running low emotionally, I go to a Mamas in Biz gathering to reconnect. And recently I decided to join the gym again. Coming home all sweaty in workout clothes makes me feel like I have found an important piece of myself again.

If there's one thread that runs through every chapter of my life, it's this: I love to help people. It's not something I set out to define myself by, but looking back, it's in everything I've done – in every job, every opportunity, and every moment I've felt truly myself.

Whether I was a receptionist, office manager, hostess, or even a technical worker on a campsite, I always found joy in being there for others. It was never just about the tasks – I wanted to make someone's day a little brighter. I'd write compliment notes for my coworkers on my last day, bring in homemade cake or popcorn, offer hugs, or take time to listen to someone's story. These small things felt natural to me, and often meant more than I realised.

I didn't need a fancy title to feel fulfilled. What mattered was the human connection; being the person others could count on, who greeted them with a smile and made them feel welcome. Even in unexpected roles, I gravitated toward helping, reassuring, and simply showing up with kindness. Because helping people doesn't just feel like something I do – it feels like who I am.

Meeting Amy and the Mamas in Biz community changed everything. A woman I met at a job fair told me about Amy, and after our first call, I knew I'd found the right support. Amy has a way of lifting you up and cheering you on when you're trying to rebuild. When I feel stuck, just one session with the Mamas in Biz ladies recharges me.

Being a mom is the biggest challenge and the biggest joy of my life. My son gives me purpose, even on the hardest days. I want to give him everything: football practice, school trips, visits to his grandparents, a happy home – and maybe even his first apartment someday. I want to show him that happiness is possible, that dreams are worth chasing, and that you can always start again. But above all, I want to teach him that not giving up is the way to make dreams happen.

I don't know what's next. Maybe I'll become a profitable trader, full-time CEO of *The Green Spirit* or a personal assistant where I can really use all my thought skills. What I do know is this: I'm on the path. I'm in the right place. And I'm grateful for every lesson along the way.

Stephanie van Steijn
@thegreenspiriteu
www.thegreenspirit.eu

GABRIELE ZILLMER

"Fear is not who you are, it's blocking you from who you really are."

In 2014, I walked away from who I thought I was. Deep inside I'm still the same, but I created the life I wanted to live; therefore, I needed to change myself to create that new life.

I grew up in Hamburg, in a middle-class entrepreneurial family, shaped by respectable bourgeois tradition. Early on, I learned to adapt.

Not to stand out, but to please others in order to receive recognition, love, and appreciation. Having my own opinion was difficult. Today, I am aware of how much fear, self-doubt, conformity, and insecurity paralysed me. I didn't believe in myself, and back then I chose the path of least resistance and stayed in my comfort zone.

At twenty-six, I started a family. Just like my mother had. At the time, I couldn't imagine any other life than that of a housewife and mother. It also included the idea that the husband provided financially for the family. For a wife to go to work was seen as unnecessary.

Isn't it easy, with such a mindset, to limit yourself and at the same time hand over responsibility? Honestly, for me, it was a mix of convenience, self-doubt, and fear of not being able to do more.

I had always dreamed of having my own business. My mother laughed at me a little and couldn't understand my ambitions. When my children got older, I began training as a naturopath. I'm interested in how our body works and what keeps it healthy and vital.

Yes, I had a good life. Until the day my husband's company went bankrupt and the house of cards collapsed.

I opened my own practice in Hamburg. Back then, I wasn't in a position to support my family financially in that difficult situation. Both children were in university. Our world fell apart for all of us.

The father of my children did everything within his power to give us the best possible life. For that, I am very grateful. I know now what it feels like to be left with nothing. Not knowing how to pay to live.

What do you do in such a situation? You learn to survive day by day, you look for solutions, you have hopes – and yes, there were family and friends who helped.

One thing became increasingly clear to me: my life couldn't go on like this, and I saw no future in my marriage.

I began to understand that blows of fate can be a call to change our situation and the key to further development. I started asking questions and becoming honest with myself.

Step by step, I began a journey back to myself.

We have all experienced some kind of trauma. Back then, I didn't understand what was happening to me, until I came across Bob Proctor and completed one of his trainings: *Thinking Into Results*.

Through this course, I realised how deeply our childhood shapes us. How much influence society, religion, family, culture, and belief systems have on us to shape who we are. How important it is for a child to be loved unconditionally, to be praised, and to be encouraged.

It taught me what an immense influence our early childhood experiences and conditioning have on our subconscious mind. From that, behavioural patterns develop that can either serve us or be destructive. To change destructive behaviours, you first need to recognise them and consciously engage with them.

The good news is: everyone can do it.

Is it easy? Not necessarily. You have to be patient with yourself. It doesn't happen overnight.

When you focus on creating a significant, lasting change in your underlying beliefs and thought patterns, you can then change your results. You create a vision of your future by combining your thoughts with feelings. This is how you can manifest the life you want to live.

Listen to the quiet voice within you. It whispers to you. In silence, you hear it the loudest.

You can ignore it, but it doesn't fall silent. It speaks from your heart. It's like the known phrase, 'listen to your heart'.

Often, we're so caught up in everyday life that we don't hear our inner voice – or we distract ourselves with trivial things.

At a certain point, I could no longer avoid this inner voice.

Every morning, I would look at myself in the mirror. Deep inside, I knew I had to make a fundamental decision in my life. For a long time, I postponed that decision because I didn't know how I or my family would cope with it, but I knew it was necessary to save myself and also my family.

In 2014, I was finally ready to make that decision. I was ready to give up my old, familiar life – whatever the cost might be. Not knowing how I would earn my own living, not knowing where I would live or how I would finance everything.

What I did have was a deep sense of trust. I also felt I had nothing left to lose. I was standing at a turning point in my life. I wasn't aware of the magnitude at the time.

Only in retrospect can we connect the dots and recognise that every decision we make leads us in a certain direction. With every decision we make, change becomes possible. It lies in our hands.

Today I know that my decision created space for something new. Then things happen that we consider magical.

It was a leap into total uncertainty – but with the certainty that I would make it. Only the *how* was not entirely clear to me.

The 'new' came unexpectedly, completely out of the blue. At my uncle's funeral, I met an old acquaintance from my youth again. We fell in love, and this led me to Copenhagen. Could I have ever imagined living in Denmark? Not in the slightest.

What I have learnt is this: *The more you are connected with yourself and feel secure in that connection, the more miracles happen – miracles we never thought possible.*

I know what it feels like to be left with nothing – when everything falls apart. My marriage had broken down. I was financially at rock bottom. Not only did I lose my home – but so did my children. My entire life was dismantled at fifty years old. Not because I wanted it that way, but because there was no other choice.

You don't have to wait until everything falls apart. Be honest with yourself. Look at what you can change – where you want to take new paths. Be courageous and don't stop walking that new path. Opportunities and doors will always open.

Life is development. Stagnation is regression.

Often, we cling to moments – even when they no longer serve us. *Freedom begins when you free yourself from constraints.*

Freedom begins with your thoughts. Thoughts trigger feelings and emotions. These, in turn, influence your actions.

I began to think differently – to truly think. I began to observe myself and realised what kind of mental carousel I had trapped myself in.

Then things happen that you could hardly have imagined possible.

How powerful is that?! We have it in our own hands to shape our lives.

What does my life look like today? I'm living the life I once dreamed of – together with my partner. We have a shared business that allows us to live in Copenhagen, Barcelona, and other places.

I have my own business in the health and wellbeing space. I'm an expert in the field of longevity, cell rejuvenation, and beauty from the inside out. I help people live healthy, fulfilled lives. With the help of preventative steps, we can lay the foundation today for a better tomorrow – for ourselves and our families.

Together with my team, we are a community of people who want to create an impact. It's called the *GameChangerNation*, and we inspire health, wealth, and change in life.

It moves me to see how our community is growing – young and older people from different nationalities and professions. So many are following us.

Community is something we all long for – and a community of like-minded people. Especially when living abroad, finding connection can be a challenge.

That's how I found my way to Mamas in Biz. I saw Amy on Instagram and felt immediately welcome. And thanks to her initiative, I've met incredible people in Barcelona – people I wouldn't have met otherwise. Without it, I wouldn't have been able to share my story here today. Thank you Amy, for creating Mamas in Biz. You're amazing!

What is your vision, mission, or purpose in life?

Maybe you're starting your own business.

Maybe you're working on your dream, your path.

Or maybe... you're just looking for a change.

I've learned how important it is to build mental strength – to train our inner muscles. Because change begins outside our comfort zone.

Life *will* test you. There are highs and lows. Unexpected challenges. Doubts. There will be days when you want to give up, or when you feel completely alone.

But... what if you didn't have to stand alone?

What if you belonged to a community where you are seen, supported, and celebrated? With other people who want to unlock their full potential, grow together, and build something meaningful?

If this resonates with you, then: *Don't stand alone. Stand with us.* This is a culture where nothing is perfect - but everything is open for improvement. Where gratitude, passion, and growth lift us higher.

If you're ready for that... then you already belong.

Whether your heart is calling for more freedom and growth through building your own business, or you simply want to take charge of your health and see where you stand today, this is your invitation.

Fear is not who you are – it's only what's blocking you from becoming who you really are.

Gabriele Zillmer
@gabrielezillmer

MARTHA NASIROV

"Every encounter can be a springboard toward our deepest mission."

I was born in Paris into an ordinary family. On the surface, my childhood looked traditional, yet it often felt empty of meaning, even though my parents did the best they could. From a very young age, I carried a strange feeling, as if I didn't quite belong. It was like watching life through a pane of glass. I felt everything – joy, tension, the weight of unspoken silences. I absorbed it all, like a sponge. And yet, no one seemed to notice. It was as if I were invisible.

People spoke about me in the third person – "she's too slow," or "not fast enough" – but never as the child they were hoping I'd be. I remember my silence, the hours I spent observing, listening without speaking, watching without intervening. It wasn't shyness. I simply didn't know how to express what was happening inside me. My body felt too narrow to contain my soul. I had been sent here with a mission, it seemed, but no instruction manual.

Very early on, a question took root in me, echoing like a silent refrain: *Why am I here?* That question became my constant companion, a breath that never left me.

I wasn't unhappy, but I was alone. Alone in the middle of others. Alone with my feelings, my questions, my strange intuitions. At school, I was set apart – not an outcast, but never fully in the centre either. I didn't need a crowd; one or two sincere friendships were enough. Noise, small talk, the social game – they exhausted me.

For a long time, I believed my difference was a flaw – an imperfection to fix, something to hide.

And yet, others always came to me. Children, adults, even strangers. They confided their secrets, fears, and wounds without me asking. It was as though my presence invited them to lay down their burdens without fear. I didn't understand why, or what to do with it all. But I was there – silent, whole, present. And somehow, that was enough.

As I grew older, I tried to fit into the mould. I chose 'normal' studies and built a career in tourism. Why tourism? Perhaps because I was fascinated by the unknown – new cultures, unfamiliar faces. Or maybe because it was something people around me could easily understand. A reassuring, respectable label.

On the outside, I was travelling, building a stable life. But inside, something was missing. Like a sacred fire I couldn't quite ignite.

Then, at twenty, I met love – the deep, transformative kind. The man I chose, who also chose me. My mirror, my life companion. With him, I learned what it meant to be truly seen. To be loved for who I was – not for what I did, or how I appeared, but for my essence. He taught me to open, to express myself, to flourish.

We met in the year 2000, in Turkey. Six years later, we left France for Switzerland – an important step in our life together. There, we built a family. Three extraordinary children came into our lives – unique, powerful, luminous souls. Through them, I discovered an even vaster love, unconditional and infinite. But with it came immense responsibility. And as often happens on paths of awakening, life found ways to shake me.

Let's go back a little...

At twenty-eight, I lost my father suddenly, without warning. The shock left an immense void, a dull but piercing grief – and also a new clarity. I realised how quickly life can end, sometimes before we have even truly lived.

Two years later, in Switzerland, I became a mother for the first time. As if my father's death weren't enough, my eldest daughter nearly left us during her first months of life. The birth was traumatic, followed by months of vague diagnoses, alarming delays, and endless medical alerts. I felt lost, exhausted, broken. Each day I was afraid – afraid of losing her, afraid I wasn't enough, afraid I would fail as a mother.

Yet in the middle of that storm, an unsuspected strength rose within me. A certainty: I had to change my life. I could no longer live how I was. I didn't want to just survive – I wanted to truly live. I needed time, freedom, and the ability to be fully present for my child.

So I made a radical choice: I quit my salaried job and stepped into entrepreneurship. I wanted to become a master of my time, to create my own reality. It wasn't comfortable, but it was vital. I believed it would be simple – that I could balance motherhood and work with ease. But reality hit hard. Loneliness, doubt, fatigue, lack of recognition, judgment from others. Nothing was easy.

But, I never gave up. Because deep down, I knew. I knew this struggle had meaning. I knew I was realigning with who I truly was.

I threw myself into transformation. I read. I studied. I experimented. I failed, doubted, and began again. I discovered personal development, spirituality, neuroscience, conscious parenting, and so much more.

I learned to meet myself. To face my shadows. To welcome my wounds. To heal. I learned to set boundaries, to say no, to say yes. To honour myself by meeting my own needs.

I discovered that my hypersensitivity was not a burden, but a gift. That my difference was my strength. That my intuition was worth more than any diploma.

I reconnected with that silent little girl inside me and told her: *I have found you. Now, you can speak.*

And suddenly, everything made sense – the gift of listening, the ability to sense the invisible, the need to create connection, the fire to share, the role of guide I had carried unknowingly since childhood.

My mission was clear: to mentor, to support, to guide, to awaken. Not as a facade or a job title, but as a vocation, a way of being. I chose to walk alongside parents to help them be happy. Because I know.

I know what it is to love until you can't breathe.

I know what it is to want to do everything right and still feel lost.

I know what it is to forget yourself in the name of love.

And above all, I know this: everything begins with us. If we want free, conscious, joyful children, we must first be that ourselves. Children don't do what we say – they become who we are. It is our vibration that guides them.

In 2019, guided by our thirst for discovery, my family and I moved to Barcelona. In the midst of the global crisis, we co-founded the *Ecole 2 Accomplissement (School 2 Accomplishment)*. A school without walls, but with strong foundations. Digital, yet profoundly human.

A school that brings together parents from all walks of life, expatriates or not, determined to take back the reins of their lives, to find balance between heart, mind, body, and soul – and to create harmony between time, money, and health.

We offer many workshops, trainings, resources, and transformative journeys around conscious parenting, emotional regulation, holistic health, balance between professional and personal spheres, and even financial security.

Our goal is simple: to give parents the keys to their own fulfilment, so their children can grow up in homes where love, awareness, and harmony reign.

What we are building is bigger than a programme or a method. It is a movement. A gentle revolution. A new reality where education no longer stops at the classroom but is lived in every gesture, every look, every choice, every silence.

Because a fulfilled parent is a complete parent, and a happy parent raises a happy child.

In 2025, my meetings with Mamas in Biz opened the doors to an international network of visionary entrepreneurs. This experience broadened my horizons and reminded me of something essential: we are not alone. Every encounter can be a springboard toward our deepest mission.

I am Martha. French by birth, Swiss by life, citizen of the world by choice. Mompreneur, zebra soul, coach, therapist, traveller, investor, free woman.

I have chosen to live fully. To love passionately. To share openly. To help create a more conscious world – one home at a time.

Today, in Barcelona, I feel at home. Here, I've found balance between family, mission, and freedom. My journey has led me exactly where I needed to be. And now, it is my turn to walk beside other parents on their path.

I believe you already carry everything you need inside you. Even when you doubt. Even when you feel alone. Even when you feel lost. This is not an end – it is a beginning.

Your story is important. Your pain has meaning. Your light deserves to shine. Never forget: your children don't need a perfect parent. They need you – fully alive.

So I extend my hand. To walk with you. To create together a life aligned, joyful, and powerful. A life where you are in your rightful place, so your children can find theirs.

Take care of yourself. Above all, make yourself your priority. Your children will thank you for showing them the way.

Martha Nasirov
@ecole2accomplissement
www.ecole2accomplissement.com

CRISTINA AQUINO

"If home were a feeling, what would it feel like for you?"

Finding home... Professionally, I am an architect and a real estate broker. In my own words: a dream weaver, weaving realities with love, faith, and purpose. I create and sell dream homes to families all day, but I myself have been haunted by the question: *Where is home?*

If home were a feeling, an emotion, how would you describe your home? Breathe in softly, take this moment and think about this: what is your feeling of home? Breathe out, gently closing your eyes.

For me, finding my home is about belonging. It feels relaxed, safe, no need to hide, no need to pretend I have it all under control. Because it doesn't matter what others think – when I'm home, I am home. Comfortable, relaxed, and at peace.

This may sound simple, but for me it has been a lifelong journey. Everywhere I go, my body asks: *Is this home? Do I feel safe here? Do I feel loved? Do I belong? Is it okay to kick back and relax? Is it okay to be myself here?*

We navigate through life making the best out of our circumstances, or this is how I feel it has been for me. I grew up in the Dominican Republic as an only child with a bipolar single mom. A loving mom, nonetheless, but it made me feel very responsible from a young age. Subconsciously, I behaved in ways that would make me feel safe. I felt that if my mom went nuts (as would sometimes happen), the boat could sink. I didn't understand it as an illness until I was seventeen, when she was diagnosed. She was loving, responsible, and appeared to live a normal life, but her struggles with mental health - let's call them 'mood swings' - kept me on alert. I became the well-behaved child trying to prevent explosions.

In 2003, at twenty-seven, I moved to Barcelona to study for my master's degree, or at least that was the official excuse. Deep down, I knew I was free to explore the world and find my home. Landing in Barcelona was fantastic! Those first years as a student and young adult were full of joy and new experiences.

In 2009, I met a lovely man. We had a good relationship and lived together. We found a place and settled down. We married, you know that song? I thought I had found my home.

We wanted a family and eventually went through *in vitro* for my first pregnancy. It was, probably surprising to most, an exciting and pleasant experience. When we received the positive pregnancy test results, at the same time we also received the confirmation that my husband would be relocated to Miami, Florida. Changes seem to always come in groups. I was thirty-eight, pregnant, and moving to the United States.

This was my husband's American dream coming true... and for me, it was going back to a place I knew, where I had lived the first two years of my life – and where I had friends and family. Was I going back home?

Both my daughters were born in Miami. We became a family there, and within three years, not only had we relocated, but we had moved house four times with babies in tow. Moving is a major life-changing experience – they say it usually takes a year to settle after a house move or relocation... we had done this to excess... I had feelings of loneliness, sadness, and, I would say, tenderness.

We decided, after the birth of my second daughter in 2017, to return to Barcelona. We landed back in Barcelona on the 20th of May, 2018 – back to our common life, friends, and our home. But I still wasn't happy. Barcelona wasn't the problem; it ran deeper than that.

In Joe Dispenza's words, many of us often live from 'object referral'. This means allowing external circumstances like jobs, relationships, and material possessions to define our happiness. But true fulfilment comes from 'self-referral' – connecting with our inner compass, knowing our values and beliefs, and living in alignment with them. That's when we stop being shaped by the world around us and start defining ourselves from within.

In May 2024, my husband and I started the separation process, while keeping a positive relationship as co-parents. I was beginning a new life with my daughters – and we call ourselves the 'Three Bees'. We each have our own superpowers and weaknesses, but together, like bees, we make everything work! That's my intention, my mission, and my goal.

From a place of gratitude, I embarked on this journey where I am the captain of the ship, determined not to let it sink. From a place of love and coherence, I chose to step into my happy self, after all, how could I teach my girls to live joyfully if I wasn't happy myself?

I was learning to re-parent myself – to love myself first, to make myself my priority. Every day it would get a little easier, until it started to feel normal.

In April 2025, I planned a trip with my girls to the Dominican Republic for three weeks, followed by one week in Miami. My intention for this trip was to tie a thread between Barcelona, the Dominican Republic, and Florida. I had a vision for my life going forward, and I wanted to somehow create a link between my three 'homes'. I didn't know how exactly, but deep inside, I trusted it was possible.

We boarded the plane. Everything went as planned. I was present and living the moment, with no worries about the future or the past, I was just being.

One morning in the Dominican Republic, the 'Three Bees' went to the beach with family. Sunshine, laughter, delicious food, and bonding – it felt good. Everyone was relaxed and in 'holiday mode'. And so was I, although I had my eyes and ears open for any clue that might get me closer to my goal of tying the thread between my three 'homes'. Then one appeared, with a sign that read: OPEN HOUSE.

Curious, I chose to follow the sign. A Canadian agent showed us a beautiful beach villa in the most luxurious resort in the Dominican Republic. I listened to his amusing stories about the property, about himself, and the resort.

I said, "I'm an architect and real estate broker, and would love to build synergies with you."

"Oh, for that you would need to speak Spanish," he said.

"Wonderful. I'm from the Dominican Republic originally, so Spanish is my first language."

"That sounds great!" He continued, "You would also need a place to stay when you're here."

"That's perfectly fine, we have a family home here." Two out of two, I thought to myself with my heart smiling.

"Fantastic, then you need to meet Crista, the manager. You must meet her in person though, it wouldn't work to meet her remotely," he added. "You need to get along with her. She only comes here once a month. She lives in West Palm Beach."

To my own surprise it dawned on me: *I already was, and had, everything I needed*. West Palm Beach would be my destination the following week. This was my moment of glory. "Splendid! Please connect us; I'll be in West Palm Beach next week and will go see her."

In that instant, I realised I'd been searching for 'home' outside myself – for external validation of my feelings, just as Joe Dispenza describes. But as I spoke with the Canadian agent, something precious clicked into place: everything I'd been seeking was already within me. *I* am home. Suddenly everything was easy and felt meant to be.

Previously, I had been looking outside for what already lived within.

We boarded the plane to Florida happy with the days spent in Dominican Republic. I was content and excited to be on the way to show Miami to my girls. This was our home when they were born. We arrived at my dear aunt and uncle's house – they had been living in the same house for many years. I had lots of childhood memories in their home. When I was pregnant with my first daughter, we celebrated my baby shower there. Then Thanksgiving and Christmas. Their home also feels like home.

We were content: my girls were happy (they had kittens to play with!), and I was pleased to be there. I couldn't wait to drive by our former house and meet our dear neighbours and friends from back when my girls were born.

We did this the next day. Driving on US1, as we got closer to our former house, I started remembering the buildings, the shops, the street view... and I felt mixed emotions. On one side, I was thrilled to show

Miami to my girls, on the other side, I was re-living feelings of the sadness I had felt when I was there.

I thought I hadn't suffered postpartum depression, but I later realised that I had been depressed for at least seven years after the birth of my firstborn. I just couldn't allow myself to suffer from 'depression' because I felt I was the one responsible for keeping the ship afloat.

I kept driving, the sadness washed away with tears, and we arrived at our dear neighbour's house. How nice it was to greet her again, to walk down to Deli Lane and eat our typical lunch, to share tales with my girls, and catch up with my friend.

This moment felt like home. Happy, safe, and very relaxed.

The next day we headed to meet Crista. When we arrived, she greeted me warmly with a wide smile and shining eyes. She was easy going and full of energy. I introduced my girls as my assistants and had them sit at a table with their colouring books.

We met, we connected, we agreed on everything – the thread was being tied. Barcelona, the Dominican Republic, and Florida were sitting on the table and the thread was knotted.

The meeting with Crista was so easy, it felt so normal – even though, for my rational mind, it was so unbelievable. It felt so natural, so meant to be, it felt like home. How can this be? We'd just met.

Actually, all parts of me and my life were also sitting on that table... Did I arrive at this moment through my current job? Through my current separation process? Through my first years of existence? Through the will and joy of offering my girls the possibility to be rooted in three different places?

I felt so elevated by the emotion of such a positive meeting. It boosted my self-esteem. I felt capable, certain, calm. I was happy. I was home.

I had found home, and the magical fact was that my home is not at all linked to a physical territory in the world.

Home is within me. Home is everywhere that I get this feeling of belonging, where I feel loved, where I feel acknowledged. I make home anywhere I go, because I am home.

Home is emotion. It's inside me. Home is my soul. Home goes with me everywhere I go, because finding home means I feel safe, comfortable, relaxed, and at peace with who I am.

I belong where I am.

"Be happy for no reason, like a child. If you are happy for a reason, you're in trouble, because that reason can be taken from you."
Deepak Chopra

If home is a feeling, an emotion, how does it feel to be in your home?

My worth, your worth, is not earned, it is owned.

Cristina Aquino
@cristina_aquino_space
www.spacearchitecture.eu

JUDI OSHOWOLE

Written by Ruairí Ó Donnchadha, her life partner.

Judi's last name, Oshowole, comes from Yoruba, West Africa. 'Osho' means the magic man, 'Wo' means to enter, and 'Ele' means the house. So, her name means 'the magic man enters the house'. I believe that Judi carried her magic within her wherever she went and left a part of that magic in every house she entered.

One afternoon in 1993, while exploring the rundown area of the Raval neighbourhood in Barcelona, I had the good fortune to see a small poster outside a restaurant in Carrer Sant Rafael. It was advertising an evening of Nigerian food and music with an exhibition of African art, and I was immediately interested. I returned to the restaurant that evening and sampled all the wonderful dishes on offer. I was curious to know who had made the delicious food.

That's when I first saw Judi Oshowole as she went from table to table talking to the other customers. I managed to get her attention and asked her to explain the different dishes and the ingredients that went into them. We continued chatting for a while, and I asked her where and when she would organise her next event. She said it would be soon, and she gave me the name of the Miami Bar in the Barrio Gótico where she was planning to have her next Nigerian night. I gave her my telephone number and told her to let me know when it was going to be because with me she had a definite customer.

In later years, Judi often teased me that I couldn't remember the names of the dishes I ate on that first occasion however, to this day I clearly remember the beautiful, flowing blue dress with a traditional Nigerian pattern she wore that night. She was charming and passionate as she spoke with her surprisingly deep voice, given her slight build. She had her hair in short twists that fell to her shoulders, and she conversed easily with all of the other customers.

At the end of that evening, I went home with my mouth still tingling from the combination of unusual spices and fiery West African hot pepper. I was looking forward to the next chance to eat more Nigerian food, but more importantly, the opportunity to talk to Judi again.

I didn't hear anything from her for weeks after that, so I looked up where Miami Bar was and I took to hanging out there, always asking the owner, James, about when Judi would be having her next food event there. He told me he hadn't seen her for some time, but he was looking forward to the next time she'd come back and prepare her potent 'Peppa

Soup' that was always a great success with his customers. He didn't have a number or an address for her, only that he knew she must live somewhere nearby because when she turned up for an event she always carried big pots of steaming soup straight from her kitchen.

That gave me hope that she couldn't be too far away and that I would see her again soon. But hope started to fade as the months went by, and James and his regulars still had no news of Judi's whereabouts. This was a time before the internet, mobile phones, and social media, so unless you had a physical address or landline number for someone there was little chance of getting back in touch with after a chance encounter.

What I didn't know about Judi at that point was that she'd had a very interesting and eventful life before arriving in Barcelona. Judi was the daughter of an English mother and Nigerian father. Looking at her family and the environment she grew up in, it's hardly surprising that Judi turned out to be the valiant trailblazer she was.

Her mother, Vera, had studied at the London School of Economics (LSE) and would later go on to work in GCHQ, the top-secret headquarters of British Military Intelligence, helping to crack military codes. Through one of her colleagues at LSE, Vera met Obaleke Olatunde Oshowole, a handsome young Nigerian medical student who was visiting from Germany. They fell in love and got married after a long-distance courtship while he completed his medical studies in Heidelberg.

Judi was born in London in October 1949, and the family spent the first years living there until her father, Tunde, finished his studies and qualified as a doctor.

Vera suffered a lot of racism and rejection in British society for having a mixed-race child. Young Judith was marked at that tender age by the discrimination of classmates and even by strangers in the street, and recalls once hearing other children shouting, "Hey, look at that black kid!" She ran back to her mother and asked in all innocence, "Mommy, Mommy, where's the black kid?" not realising they were pointing at her.

It was a moment when she realised she was black and different from other children, and not very welcome by the society she was growing up in. It was a time in Britain when it was common to see signs in the front window of lodging houses – NO BLACKS, NO DOGS, NO IRISH.

Things changed for Judi at the start of the sixties when Tunde, now a qualified doctor, took the family back to Nigeria, where the nation was preparing with euphoria for independence and was welcoming all returnees with open arms without questioning their parentage.

Her father joined the Nigerian Army. He was the first Nigerian army doctor to take over after British rule. He was posted to Ibadan in central Nigeria, and Judi started studying for her A-levels at the International School of Ibadan. She adopted the shorter version of her name after seeing the actress Judi Dench portray strong women characters in plays and films.

The sixties were a time of great change and liberty in Nigerian society, and the country was starting to flex its muscles as one of the largest and most powerful African nations. Immense oil deposits were just being discovered, and Nigeria was exerting its dominance in the world's political, economic, and musical scenes. Of course, Judi was in the middle of it all. Her parents had close friends among those Nigerian returnees who, like them, were highly educated and ambitious. They had come back to Nigeria full of hope and great dreams of rebuilding a country that had been hobbled in its development by a harsh, racist colonial power for a hundred years.

Tunde, as a prominent doctor, had many friends and colleagues both in the Army and among the rising political circles around the country. Judi was privy to some of the intense conversations her parents had with these rising stars of the nation, who would come around for drinks at her house. Though Judi, being the fun-loving person she was, would sometimes slip away in the late evening to meet up with her school friends and, despite being underage, they would hang out at Fela

Kuti's night club, 'The Shrine', to listen to Fela working on his AfroBeat rhythms that would take the world by storm in the following years.

Judi was also inadvertently at the cutting edge of fashion in Nigeria at that time. While browsing some of the trendiest clothes shops, she was asked by the owner to try on one of the hottest styles that had just arrived from Europe. A local photographer happened to be there and snapped a picture of her while she was modelling the clothes, telling her he would send her a copy by post. To her dismay (but also with a hint of secret pride, I suspect), the next day her picture appeared in the newspaper with the headline 'the first mini skirt to arrive in Nigeria'!

Her father was outraged and wanted to throw her out of the house for shaming the family – she was only saved by the intercession of her mother.

When she left secondary school, Judi was already a person of passionate opinions and a strong sense of justice. She moved to New York to do a degree in journalism at St. John's University and during that time also worked part-time in a left-wing bookshop. There she became very interested in the Black Panther movement and got to know some of the leading members who frequented the shop, in particular the highly prominent and very vocal firebrand, Angela Davis. This friendship would be memorable for both of them – Judi was inspired by Angela to fight tirelessly throughout her life for the rights of black and oppressed people. Angela would remember Judi from those times when, many decades later, Angela came to Barcelona for an official speaking engagement and gladly carved a number of hours from a hugely busy schedule to speak at a private event for Judi and her association of Black women in Barcelona (Barcelona International Black Sisters).

With her degree in journalism completed, Judi returned to Lagos, Nigeria and started writing a weekly column called *A Window on My Mind* for Nigeria's *Punch* newspaper. She also worked for a time as a travel agent in the early 1970s, and later she opened a fashion boutique before returning to the UK to do a degree in education in Birmingham.

Her son, Motolani, was born in 1974. After working as a secondary school English teacher in Birmingham, she moved to London when she got a job at Camden Council. Her first position was with the Camden Committee for Community Relations, where she supported immigrant associations that were suffering discrimination in the Government institutions. Later, she transferred to the Women's Unit.

Judi had been particularly angered by a meeting about racial harassment in a housing estate, where the victims weren't even invited to tell their side of the story at a council meeting held to resolve the situation. Camden Council workers themselves suffered institutionalised racism at work with lower pay, blocked career opportunities, and unfair dismissals. They got little help from the national union, NALGO. So Judi said, "We must start our own group," and with the help of committed colleagues set up the Camden Black Workers Group.

This would go on to be the largest Black-led Trade Union organisation in Europe, and it is still active today after more than forty years. Using 'Black' politically to include Asians as well as people of African descent, Camden Black Workers Group quickly became a force to be reckoned with, not only targeting institutionalised racism within Camden Council but also offering its support to other causes like the Miners' Strike, the Anti-Apartheid Movement, and Palestine.

Judi was a real leader, forceful and politically astute, with the fantastic quality of bringing full awareness of racism and how to stand up to it. Some of the women she forged friendships with during that time were to remain her close friends throughout her life. Judi was also a member of Camden Black Sisters and was involved with one of the most influential political movements of the day, the Organisation of Women of African and Asian Descent.

In the early 1990s, funding for race relations was cut drastically by the Tory government and Judi's section in Camden Council for race relations was closed down. That was when Judi decided to change direction and move to Barcelona to start a new life and a new career.

In Barcelona, she used her degree in education to get a job teaching English and also started hosting West African events where she would take over a restaurant or bar and sell the Nigerian dishes that she would cook. It was just at that time I had the good fortune to come across that small poster advertising one of her evenings. Little did I know at the time, it was something that was going to shape the rest of my life.

Various months had passed since we first met, and there was still no news of Judi. I continued to drop into Miami Bar occasionally, just in case luck would come my way again.

Then one evening, when it seemed like the light of an elusive twinkling star was being pulled quietly towards a far-away constellation, my telephone rang. When I picked up the receiver, there was loud old-school reggae music pulsating in the background. It was Judi calling to ask if, by chance, I still remembered her. I told her that of course I remembered her! She explained that she'd had to go back to London for a time, but now she was back in Barcelona to stay and wanted to celebrate her return with a big birthday bash and asked if I would like to come to her party. I said yes right away.

At the party, I was able to spend a lot more time talking to Judi and I realised how absolutely charming she was. She delighted in entertaining people with her food, her music collection, and her books, which she adored. She was always ready to recommend and share her books.

Before I left the party Judi picked out one book on Irish politics that she thought I would find interesting. I gladly accepted the offer of the book as it was a subject I was very interested in, but also borrowing the book meant that I would have to meet her again to give it back.

Judi always insisted on having a party for her birthday, the 12th of October – a public holiday in Spain, so everybody would be able to celebrate with her. I didn't know then that this was going to be the first of thirty birthday celebrations we would share.

We met regularly after that, and I invited her to join the English language radio programme that I worked on with other friends on the pirate radio station *Radio Contrabanda*. Her wonderful, deep radio voice and strong political views were a perfect addition to the programme. She'd worked and published as a journalist in Lagos, so she soon became a driving force in the team that produced the weekly magazine shows. Soon after that, we moved in together as our love grew.

Judi's politics were strongly left-wing, always carefully thought out and based on close observation and extensive reading of a subject. In London, she was a firebrand for equality and justice for all. She was a leader and fearless about being on the frontline of protests and demonstrations. She didn't back down when faced with the powerful racist institutions of the British government when working in London. She didn't back down when up against violent riot police during the miners' strike protests and was subsequently arrested for trumped-up charges of 'assaulting the police lines with a leather jacket and then trying to escape by jumping over a seven-foot wall'. By the way, Judi was just five-foot-two!

She wasn't cowed by the Spanish authorities either when she first arrived in Barcelona. The situation of race relations in Spain in the nineties was far behind what it was in the UK. Black people were treated with suspicion or open racism in many cases. After spending a night in the cells for failing to produce her passport when stopped by police in the street, Judi decided to set up Barcelona International Black Sisters (BIBS) to counter the racism and isolation experienced, particularly by Black women.

By the year 2000, we were working together with our own business in nutrition, and were very active in Barcelona's business community. In later years, Judi developed a worsening condition of chronic obstructive pulmonary disease (COPD). The disease destroys the lung's capacity to absorb oxygen and, in the later stages, requires being attached to an oxygen tank to be able to breathe. This debilitating disease never dampened her enthusiasm for supporting women with ambition and determination.

When Judi met Amy, the founder of Mamas in Biz, in April 2023, they instantly became friends. I think that Judi recognised in Amy many of the traits she felt in herself – a woman who loved supporting other women and helping them bring to the fore their inner strengths, a woman who revelled in providing a platform that promoted women's success in the world and celebrated that success with them every step of the way. Amy was also juggling a young family while pursuing her own career with Mamas in Biz in a similar way to Judi, as a single mum, had fought for her own self-fulfilment in London decades before, when living in dangerous and overcrowded government accommodation with her young son.

Amy was able to teach Judi to bridge the generational gap from the time of forty years previously, of tapping out her journalistic messages on a Remington, to promoting her business by posting on Instagram from her Samsung. Judi loved the community of strong entrepreneurial young women Amy had created and attended the Mamas in Biz events as often as her failing health would allow.

Despite having to wear an oxygen mask with a tank, and use an electric wheelchair in her final years, she cheerfully defied the doctors' grim prognosis. She magically fought her way out of a dangerously low health situation and bounced back ready for the next adventure.

We toured Spain, travelled to France, and attended a family reunion in Ireland with a double beer-barrel-sized oxygen tank in tow. In the face of the challenges, Judi continued to live life to the full.

Sadly, on the 5th of July, 2024, in Barcelona, Judi's spirit broke away from the constraints of her physical body and was able to fly free as a swallow in the summer sky. While the loss of her love and companionship is something I will always mourn, I delight in the fact that I was lucky. Not only lucky once, when I saw that poster advertising her Nigerian event in the Raval, and not only twice, that I was around to answer her call that evening she phoned to invite me to her party, but that I was extremely lucky to be in the presence of her magic for thirty years of my life.

Judi Aderinola Oshowole
12th October, 1949 – 5th July, 2024

Founder of black workers group was 'a real leader who stood up to racism'

OBITUARY

Judi Oshowole: 'a real leader, forceful and astute'

WHENEVER Camden Black Workers Group founder Judi Oshowole looked back on her more than eventful life, it was a private audience with civil rights heroine Angela Davis that remained one of her most cherished moments.

Judi, who has died aged 74, arranged the meeting in 2017 as head of Barcelona International Black Sisters (Bibs), an organisation she set up after moving to the city 30 years previously. Davis, who was in Barcelona for a speaking engagement, spent 90 minutes to talk with Judi and other Bibs members in her free time despite her busy official schedule.

"It was a wonderful achievement," remembers Tunde Longmore who was at the meeting. "Judi somehow managed to bypass the red tape and reach out personally to Angela, but if anyone was going to pull it off, it would be Judi."

At her funeral at Tanatori del Litoral in Barcelona on July 9, family and friends attested to Judi's fighting spirit, which first manifested itself in the public realm when she ran away from primary school in Nigeria in protest at having to carry water on her head and came into her own when she threw herself into the momentous anti-[illegible] and feminist [illegible] in Camden and [illegible] during the 1980s and 90s.

One of three children, Judith Anne Aderinola Oshowole was born on October 12, 1949 to an English mother and Nigerian father in London. She spent part of her childhood in Nigeria, where her father Olatunde worked as a doctor, attending St Anne's School in Ibadan before returning to the UK for her secondary schooling. In 1966 she was back in Nigeria to complete her education in Ibadan.

Already a person of passionate opinions, in the early 1970s she wrote a weekly column for Nigeria's *Punch* newspaper called A Window on my Mind. Later she opened a boutique in Lagos before studying for a degree in education in Birmingham.

After getting a job at Camden Council, first with Camden Committee for Community Relations and then the women's unit, Judi set up Camden Black Workers Group in 1981 with Azim Hajji in response to the dearth of black voices in discussions about tackling racism.

"Judi was particularly angered by a meeting about racial harassment on the Regent's Park Estate where the victims weren't even invited. The council had no senior black housing officers so Judi said we must start our own group," recalls CBWG pioneer member, former social worker and long-time friend Janette Brewster.

Using "black" politically to include Asians, CBWG quickly became a force to be reckoned with, not only targeting institutionalised racism within the council but also offering its support to causes like the miners' strike, the Anti-Apartheid Movement and Palestine.

"Judi was a real leader, forceful and politically astute, with a fantastic quality of bringing a full awareness of racism and how to stand up to it," added Ms Brewster, who accepted a special recognition award on Judi's behalf at CBWG's annual gala at the Irish Centre last year.

By now living in Belsize Park and bringing up her son Tola alone, Judi, then known by her married name of Bashir, was also, as a member of Camden Black Sisters, involved with one of the most influential political movements of the day, the Organisation of Women of African and Asian Descent (OWAAD).

In the early 1990s the grandmother-of-two got a job teaching English in Barcelona. After spending the night in the cells for failing to produce her passport when stopped by police, she decided to set up Bibs to counter the racism and isolation experienced by black women.

As fun-loving as she was serious, she is fondly remembered for the parties she hosted at the book-lined flat she shared with husband Ruairi, just minutes away from Las Ramblas, regaling guests with her hot pepper soup and often challenging them to her favourite board game of Scrabble.

Judi frequently returned to London to help look after her mother Vera, to whom she was devoted, as well as to receive treatment for her chronic lung disease. Despite having to wear an oxygen pack and use a wheelchair in her final years, she cheerfully defied doctors' grim prognosis by continuing to live life to the full. She died peacefully on July 5 at Hospital Evangèlic de Barcelona with her family at her side.

OWAAD founder and author Stella Dadzie was the celebrant at her funeral, which was attended by almost 150 people, in person and via video link, and included the music of Sweet Honey and the Rock and Fela.

ANGELA COBBINAH

1

Camden New Journal, 25th July, 2024.

Judi & Ruairí, Mamas in Biz Pop-up Market, 2023.

Amy & Judi enjoying Irish coffee in 2023.

NATALIA HOOKER

"Your story matters too." A letter from the editor.

When we began this project, the aim was to create a book where mothers in business could be heard, celebrated, and connected. What emerged has been far richer than I imagined – a myriad of voices, cultures, and journeys that remind us of the power of sharing our stories.

Thank you Amy, for the wonderful idea to create *Connections*. You truly are a miracle worker and an inspiration to us all. And thank you to every single contributor – for sharing. In each of your memoirs, I heard my own voice. Editing your work has been a joy and a powerful reminder that *'we are one'.*

I've been a published author since 2010, but sometimes I find it ironic that I call myself a writer. In reality, I probably spend twenty percent of my time actually writing. Most of my time is spent helping other authors, editing, creating, marketing, dreaming up new book ideas... and being a single mum.

What I didn't know before reading these stories was how many of the women in Mamas in Biz are single mothers. I wouldn't trade motherhood for anything – but the reality is, motherhood is tough, and single motherhood is even tougher. There's no second income to rely on. No 'girls' night out' clause. No chance of a sleep in. You have to be the soft mama your baby needs, and the disciplinarian too.

Before becoming a mum, life felt light and breezy. I worked, saved, travelled, and lived fully. My low moments were caused by heartbreak or the yearning for a baby. Other mothers would say to me, "Your life is amazing! Why do you want a child? It's not an easy road." I heard them, but my dream of being a mum was stronger than any rational advice.

The years flew by – more work, investments, successes, boyfriends coming and going – until my body clock said, *This is your last chance...* I had been dating a lovely man, but he didn't want another child; he already had a son. I knew that if I stayed with him, I'd be giving up my dream to have a baby. We parted.

It was a complicated time. Work was changing, and my income was unstable. A tenant in my investment property stopped paying rent for six months and was a complete nightmare on many levels. I couldn't get him out. Meanwhile, I had two big mortgages. I was stressed to the max. All the while, my body clock was ticking, ticking, ticking...

It felt like my life was falling apart. They call it a midlife crisis, and perhaps that's what it was. Maybe it was hormonal? Who knows, but I woke up each morning hardly inspired to greet the day. Life used to be so fun and adventurous. *What had my life become? In my forties, single, no children, financial stress?* I couldn't do much about being forty, but I knew the other factors were things I could change.

I've always loved self-help books, and I turned to one that propelled me out of my slump. It suggested to meditate with the mantra: *Ek Ong Kar Sat Gur Prasad*. This mantra is meant to be very powerful for raising your vibration, and, while listening, you must hold positive thoughts. I had practised Kundalini yoga for many years, and the mantra resonated deeply with me. If it worked, what I thought about would come into my life at fast speed.

I found a version sung along to music on YouTube. I listened, closed my eyes, and visualised my baby in my arms, the tenant out of my life, as well as other positive images. The version I found happened to be eleven minutes, so that is what I did – eleven minutes every morning and night, and yes, things began to shift.

I felt better in a few days and fully embraced that my motherhood journey would be solo. Within a month of listening regularly, the tenant had left, and I sold the apartment two weeks later (yes, a small miracle in the Spanish market!). Then, after a few months, I was pregnant. Yay!

When my beautiful daughter was about a year old, I took the biggest leap yet and started my own business – the business I had dreamed of for years but never dared to launch. I had been working in publishing for fifteen years as an agent, and there was no greater pleasure to me than being surrounded by books, and I loved dealing with publishers. But I had the urge to create more of my own books, and books for other authors. I wanted to *be* a publisher. So, in 2021, I founded Alaya Books. I did it for myself, for my baby's future, and out of pure passion.

I was thrilled to dive into wonderful book projects. My daughter kept me busy, of course, but I put her into daycare and got to work. However, shortly after launching my business, my mother, who lives with me, was diagnosed with breast cancer. I had to start a new vocation, not only as an entrepreneur and single mum, but as a carer.

My mother and I have always been very close. We share the same love for books, and we worked together for many years in publishing. We travelled to book fairs all over the world – we were known as a team. When she was near retirement, it seemed natural that she would move from cold Poland to warm Spain so that I could be there for her. However, I'd never envisioned this.

My daughter was only one and a half when the chaos started, and I had no income other than my fledgling business. The cancer moved from her breast to her liver, and then into her lungs. Talk about life throwing a curveball. At the time of writing in 2025, my mum is still on chemo, but finally cancer free.

I share these snippets of my own journey as a way of recognising, *'You are seen, heard, and supported'.*

You're a single mum? Yes, so am I.

You've been through IVF? Yes, so have I.

You had a bad breakup? Yes, so did I. I divorced in 2009, and I would not wish it upon anyone. Even though we had no joint investments or children, it was possibly the single most devastating time of my life. The promises, the dreams, the future, all dissolved and shattered. I was left to rebuild again.

You've been a carer? Yes, so have I.

You had to defect? So did I. My mother is Polish, and when I was three, we were stuck in Poland during the communist regime, so my mum carried me and my brother into the night and fled with the help of the Australian Ambassador. We had to destroy our Polish passports and renounce our Polish citizenship. My mum didn't know when she would see her parents and sister again.

You were diagnosed with endometriosis? So was I. The doctors told me I wouldn't fall pregnant. In retrospect, I'm not sure if the diagnosis was correct, but I was suffering incredible abdominal pain.

It took you a while to find your life purpose? Me too! I was a banker and even a singer before finding my way into publishing.

You love Barcelona? Yes! Me too. Originally from Sydney, I lived in Warsaw, London, New York, Paris, and Milan before arriving in Catalonia in 2005. I haven't moved away since.

You clean up litter from the beach? So do I – especially plastic. It's wonderful to see how my young daughter naturally does the same.

You want to give back more? Yes, so do I! My dream is to set up a foundation providing food, books, and education to children in need.

So it's from a place of deep appreciation that I applaud the heartfelt and diverse stories that make up this anthology. On many levels they have been a reflection of my own experience. Through *Connections*, the Alaya Books motto rings true:

The World Needs Your Story.

To our readers, thank you for joining us. May these pages offer you connection, strength, and the reassurance that your story matters too. While our paths may differ, we are not walking them alone.

With gratitude,
Natalia Hooker

Author of *UnStuck*, *LJ Hooker The Man*, *Messages from Angels*, *Flower Book*, *Kitten Tails*, the *Misha the Travelling Puppy* series, *Wish Upon*, and *Are You?*.

@alayabooks
@alayabooksforchildren
www.alayabooks.com

PHOTOS

Mamas in Biz Meet & Hangout event, May 2025. Photo: By Mish

Mamas in Biz photoshoot, 2023. Photo: Rosa Mota

Mamas in Biz Christmas Market at Stephy's, 2025. Photo: Pauline Mattia

Mamas in Biz Meet & Hangout event, September 2025. Photo: By Mish

International Women's Day, 8th March, 2025.

Social gathering and birthday celebration, June 2025.

Mamas in Biz Instagram Marketing Workshop, St. Jordi, 23rd April, 2025.

Mamas in Biz Meet & Connect event, June 2024.

Mamas In Biz photoshoot, 2024. Photo: By Mish

Mamas in Biz Meet & Connect event, January 2024.

Mamas in Biz photoshoot, 2024. Photo: By Mish

mamas **in biz**
barcelona

ACKNOWLEDGEMENTS

First and foremost, my deepest gratitude goes to Ruairí. Thank you for accepting my proposal to dedicate this book to your late partner, Judi, who always dreamt of telling her story but sadly never had the chance. This book stands in her honour, her spirit has been present throughout the whole process, and the care with which her story has been told is a true tribute to her.

I also must thank Natalia from Alaya Books for her time, effort, and energy in supporting the women through their writing journeys, and for offering guidance and encouragement every step of the way.

Katherine Slusher, thank you for writing the wonderful Foreword and for giving feedback on the contributors' work. Thank you as well to Marina Kuperman Villatoro for your feedback, and to Vivienne Stein-Rostaing for your meticulous proofreading.

And finally, my heartfelt thanks to all the women who have joined us in creating this publication, and to everyone who has believed in this project from the very beginning, recognising the vision of Mamas in Biz and the importance of telling these stories.

With love and gratitude,
Amy

Please follow Mamas in Biz on Instagram:

Scan me

@mamasinbizbarcelona

Scan me

@mib.innercircle

Book an obligation free connection call with Amy:

Scan me

www.mamasinbiz.com

Alāya books

The world needs your story.

www.alayabooks.com

CONNECTIONS

barcelona
mamas
in biz

SEEN HEARD SUPPORTED

Printed in Dunstable, United Kingdom

70763506R00114